This fabulous book

belongs to

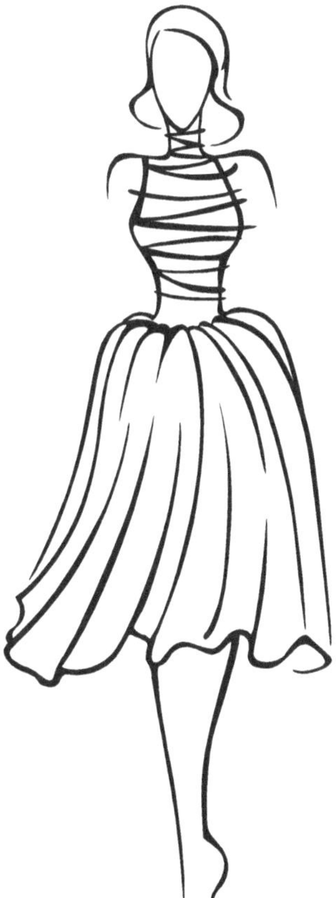

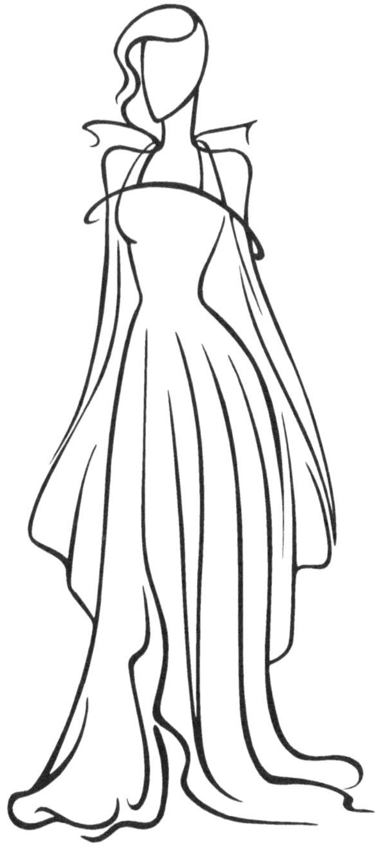

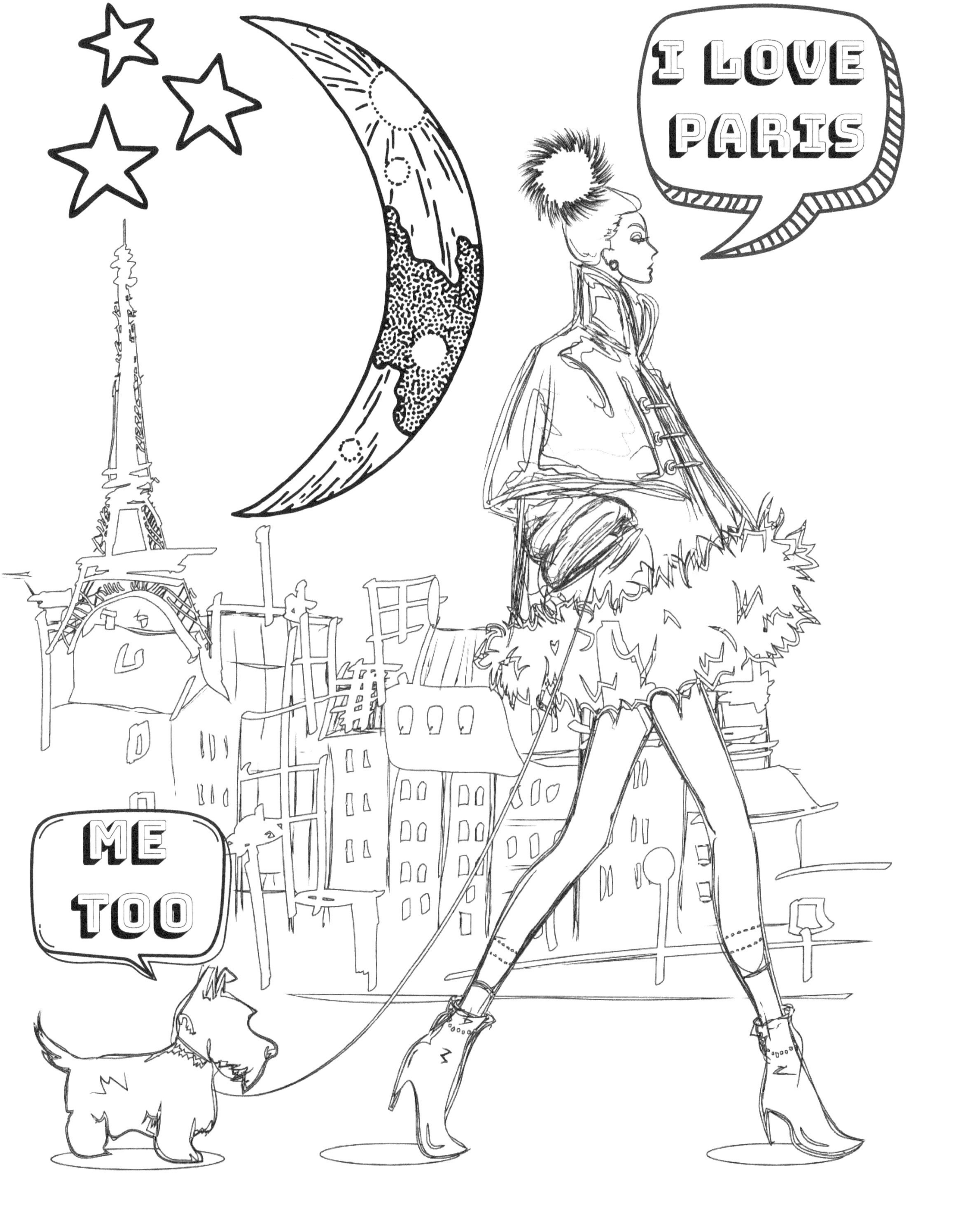
I LOVE PARIS
ME TOO

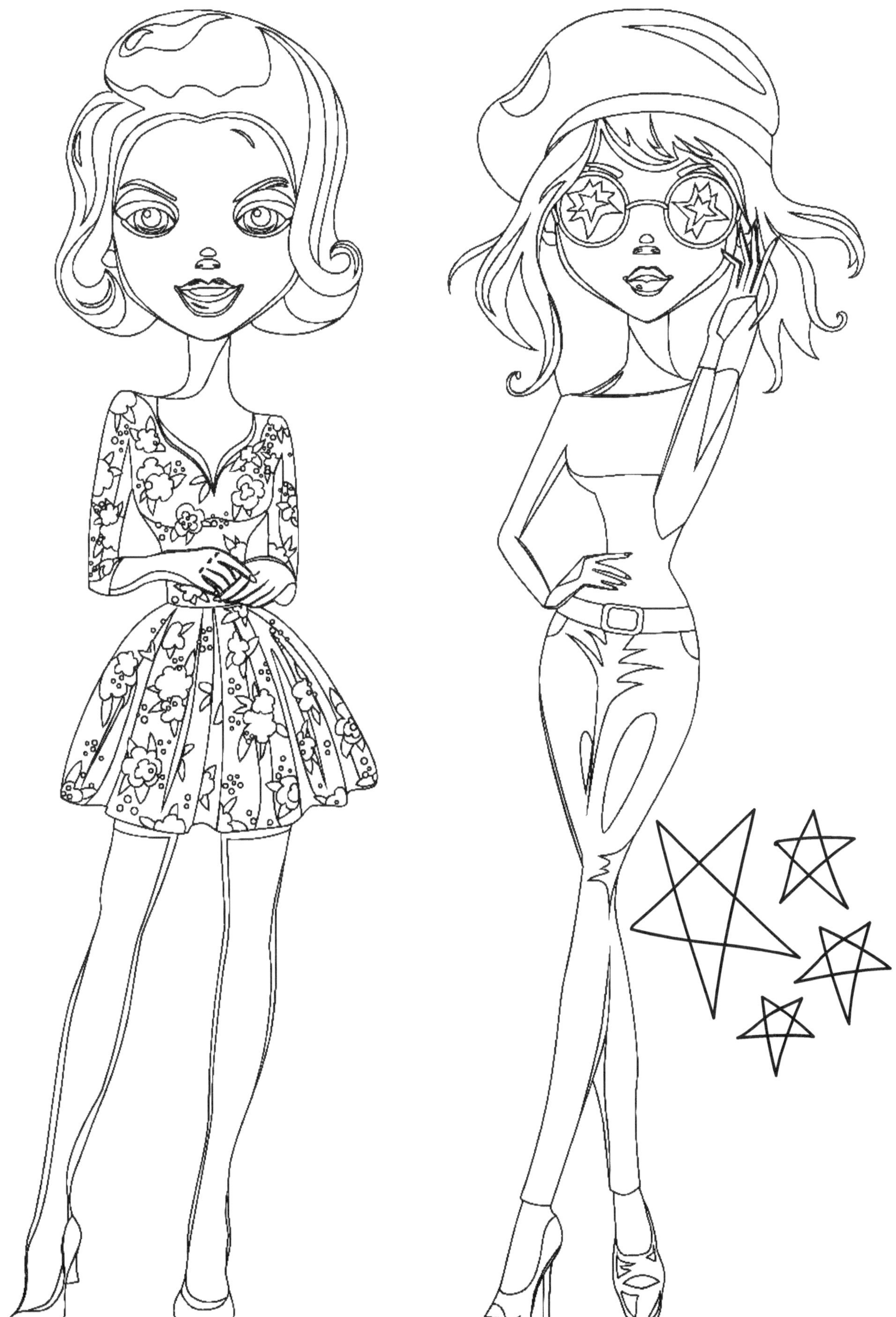

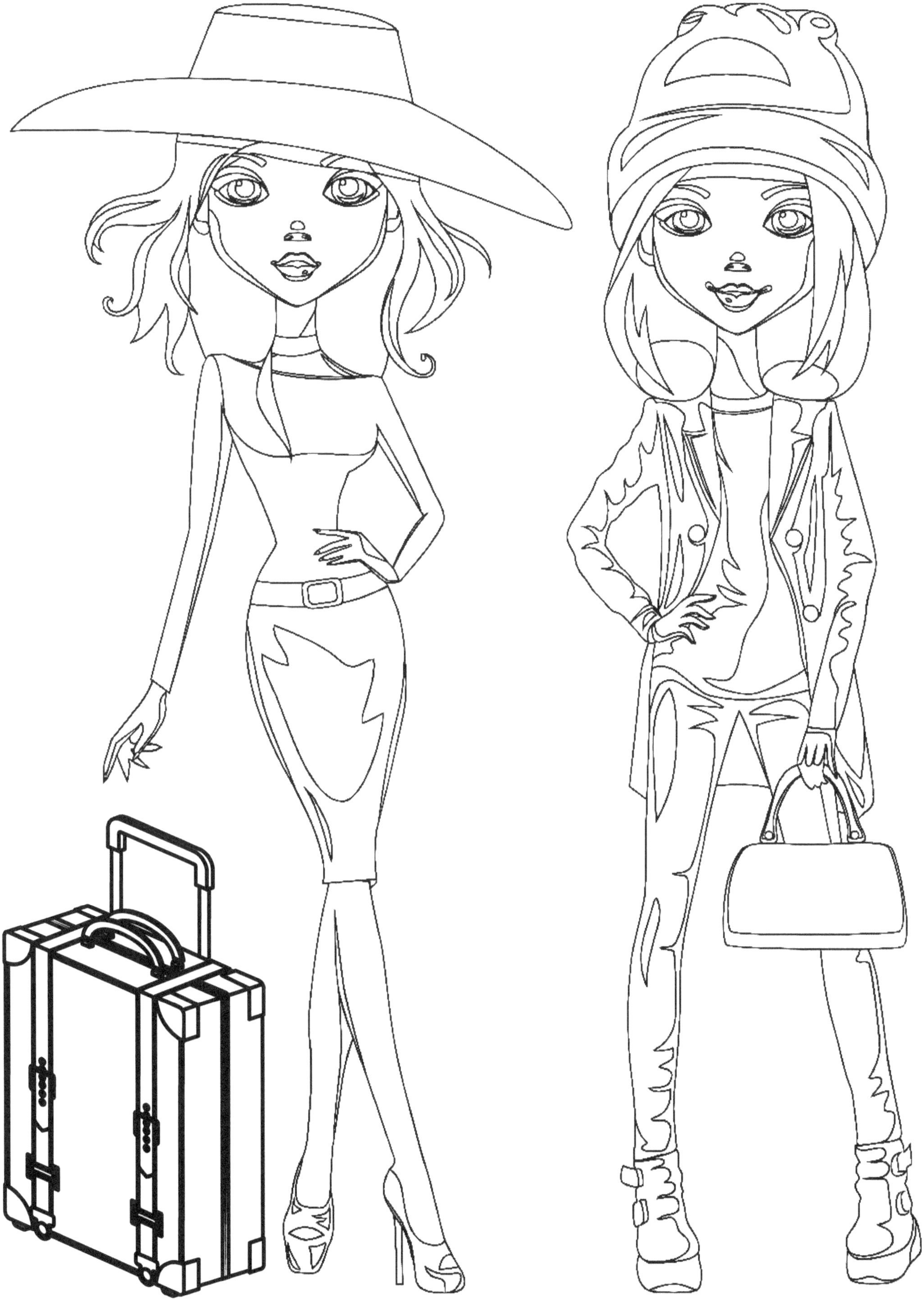

# FASHION !

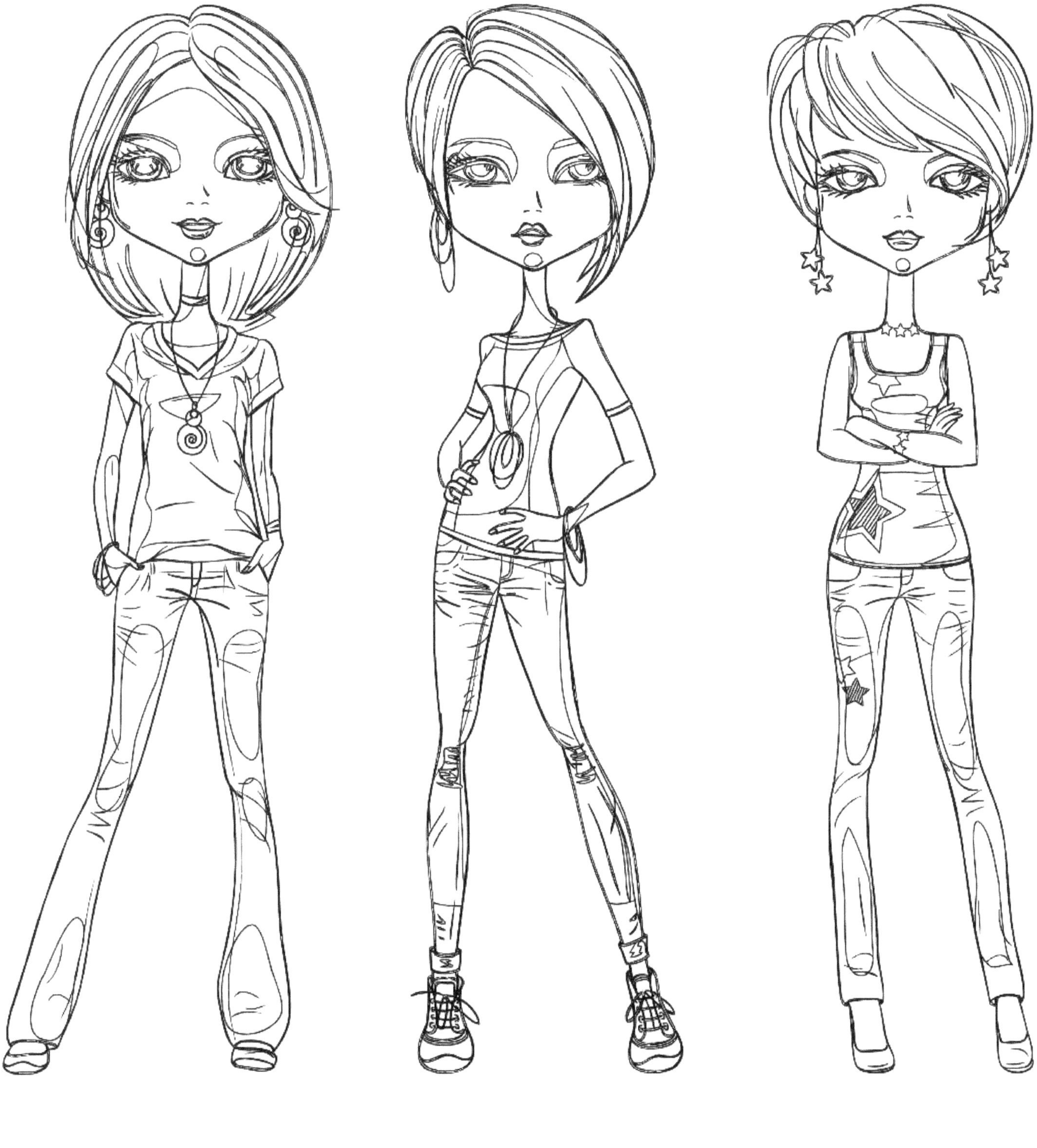

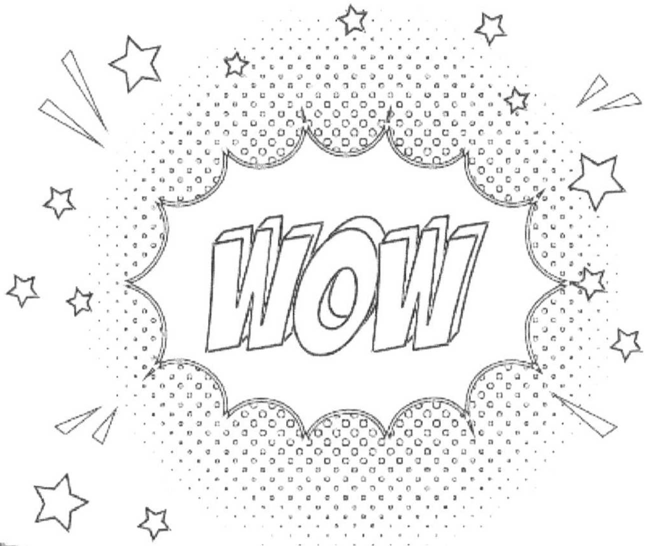
WOW

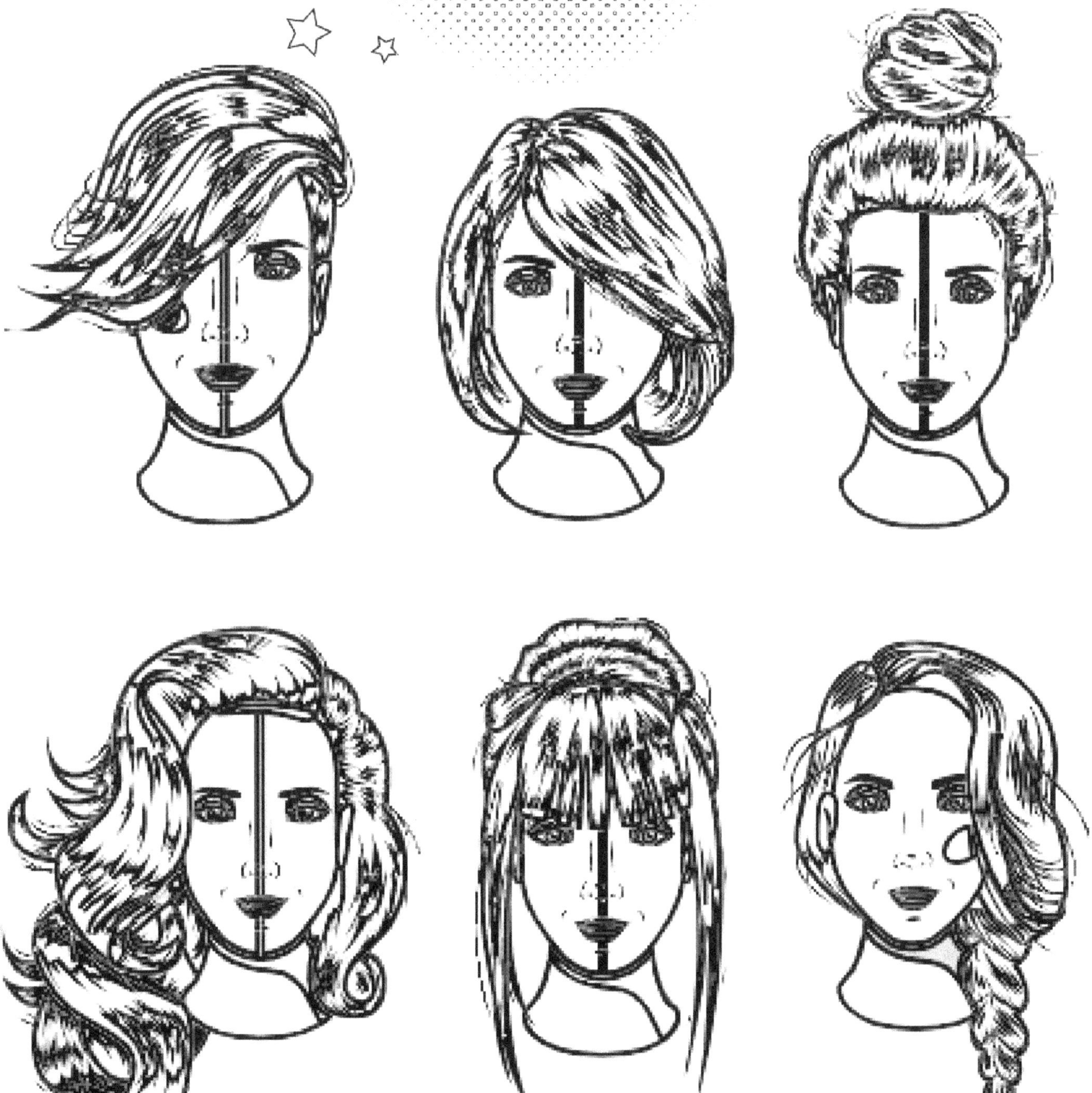

# MY BAGS

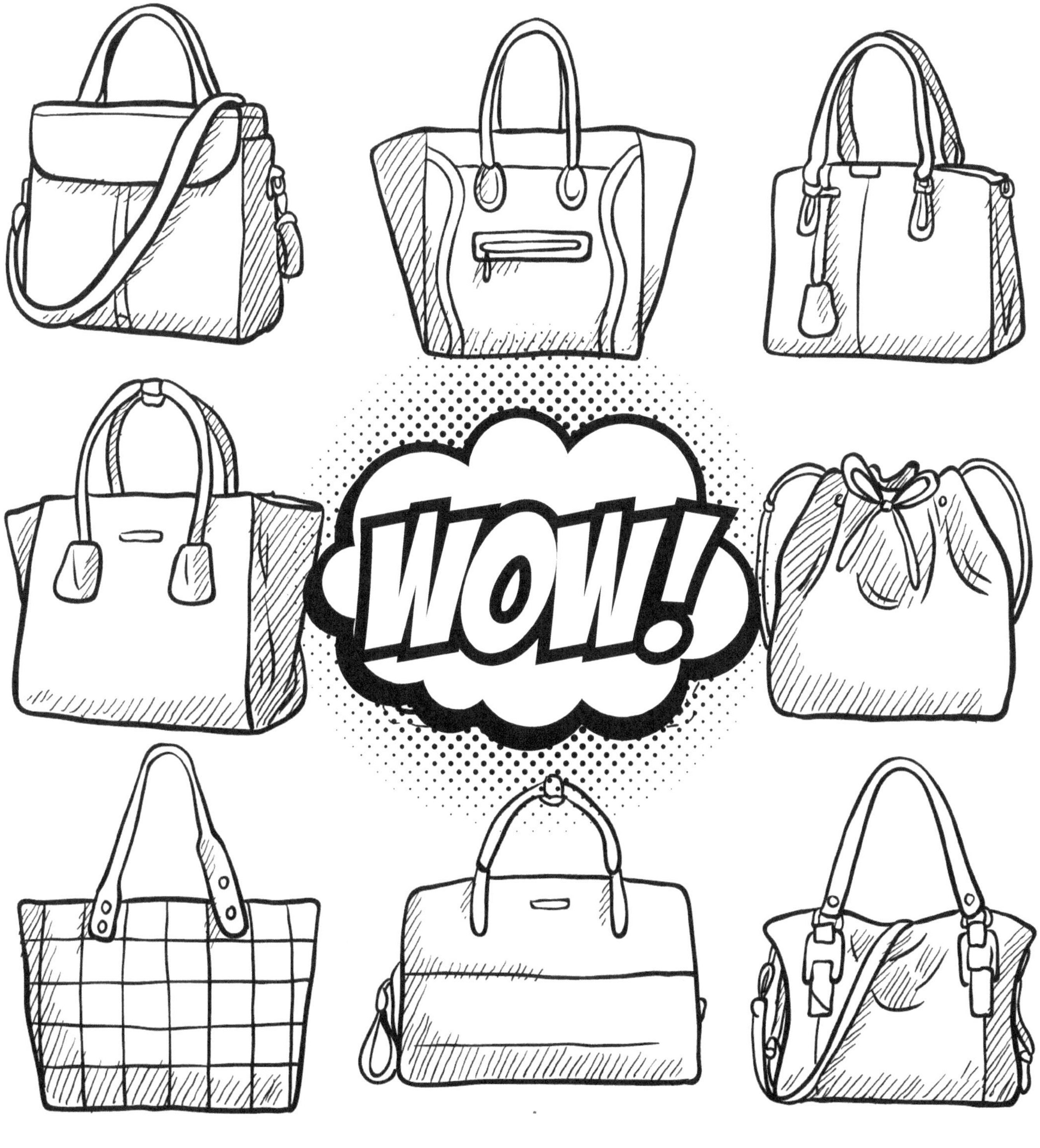

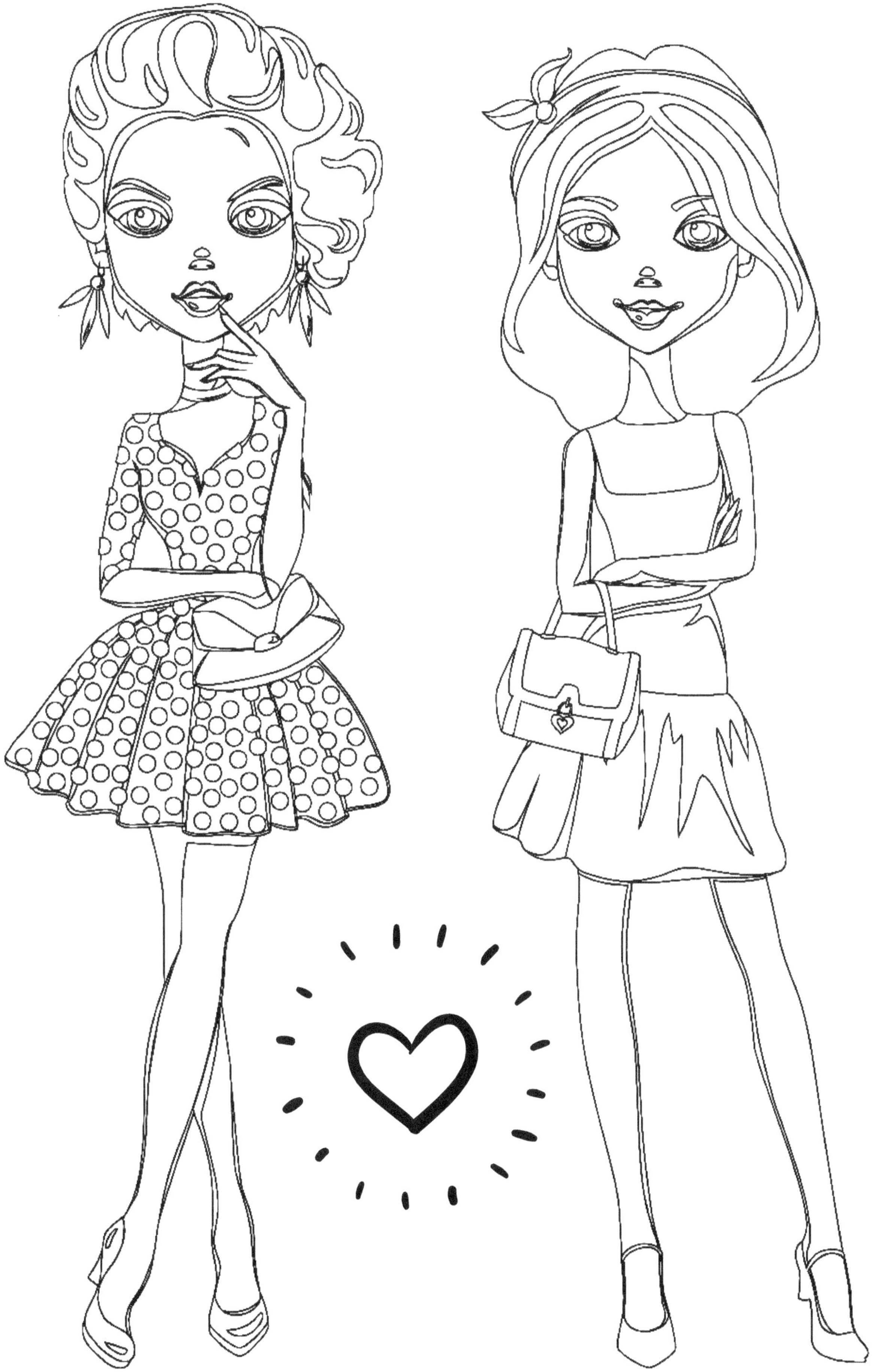

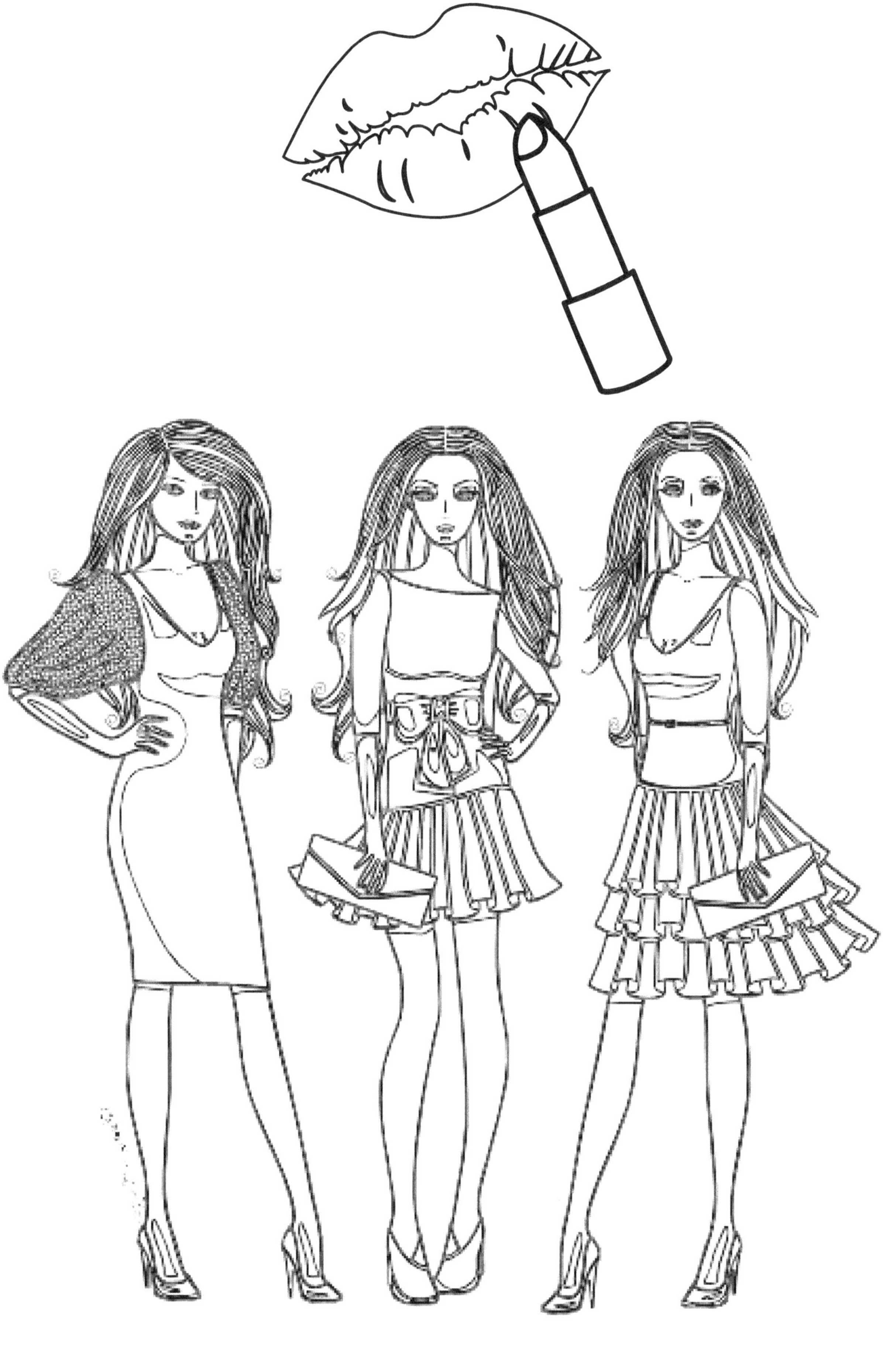

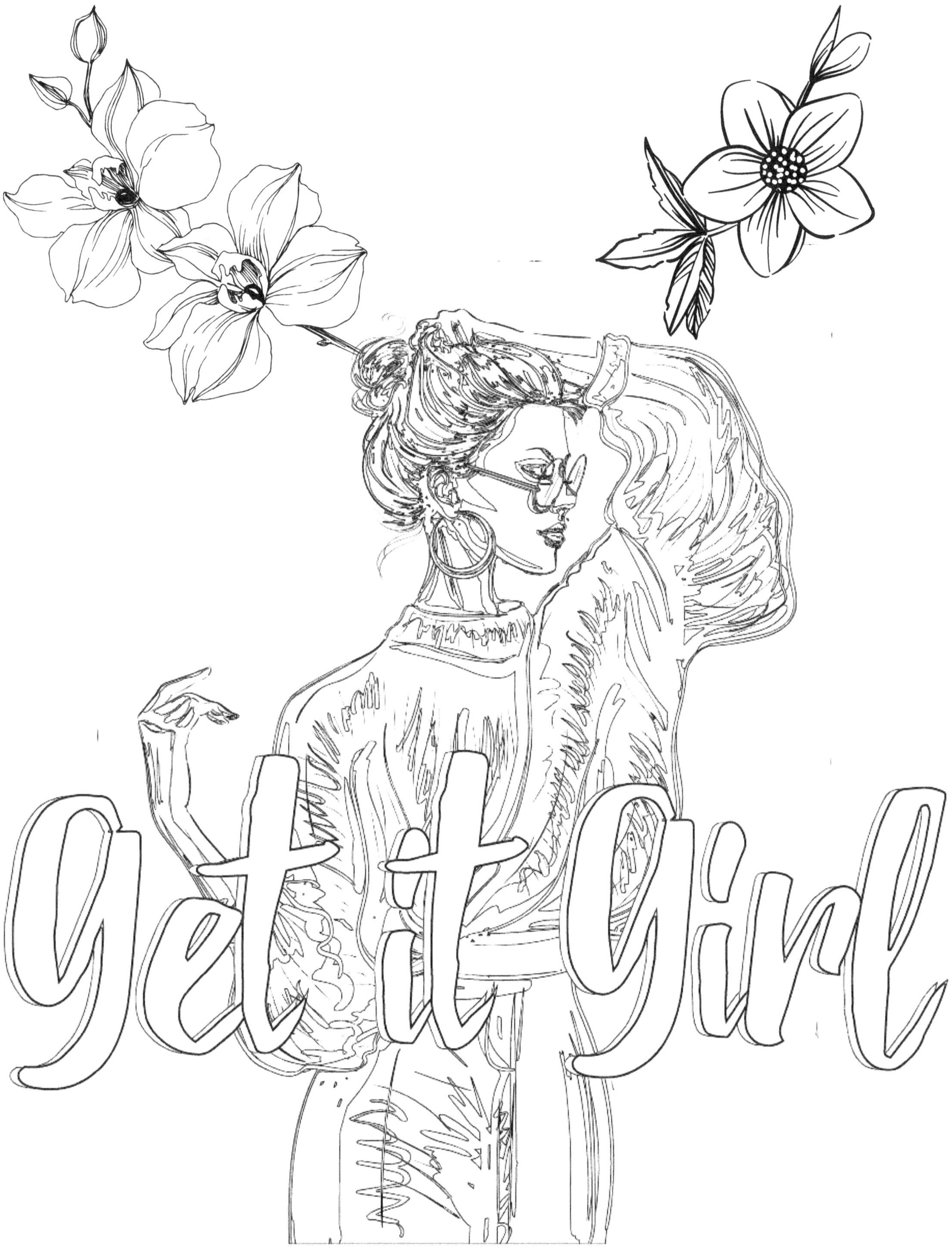
Get it Girl

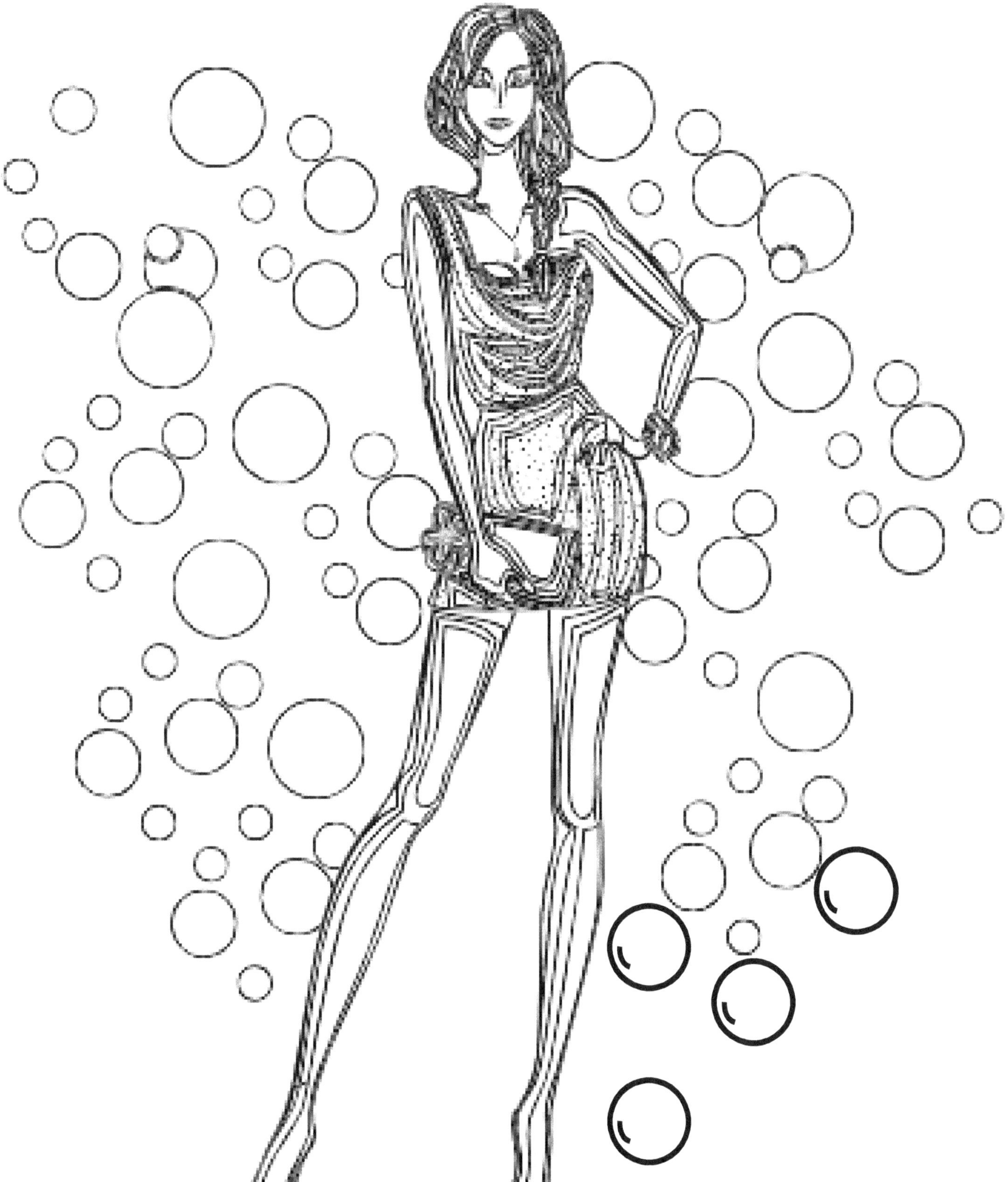

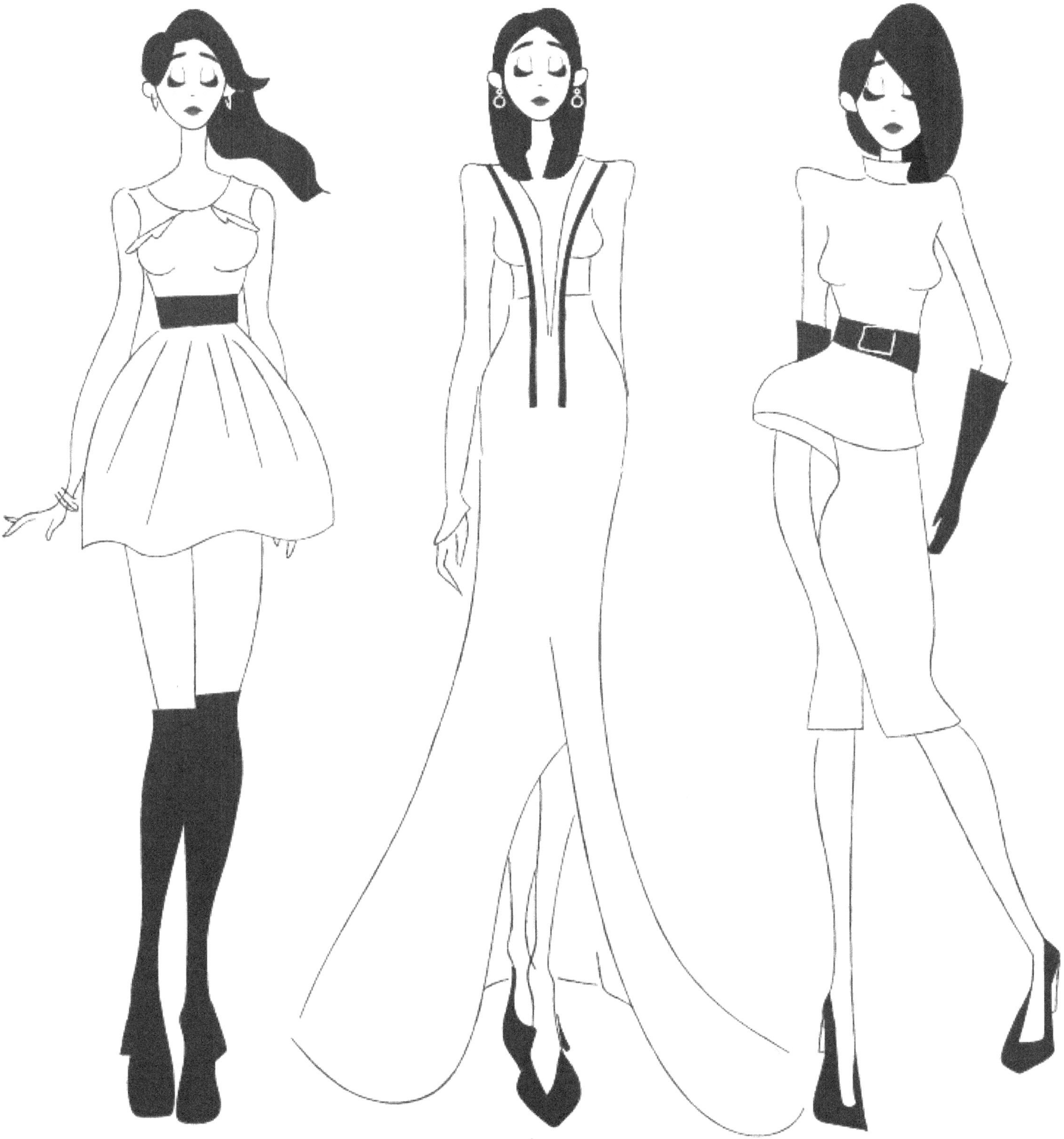

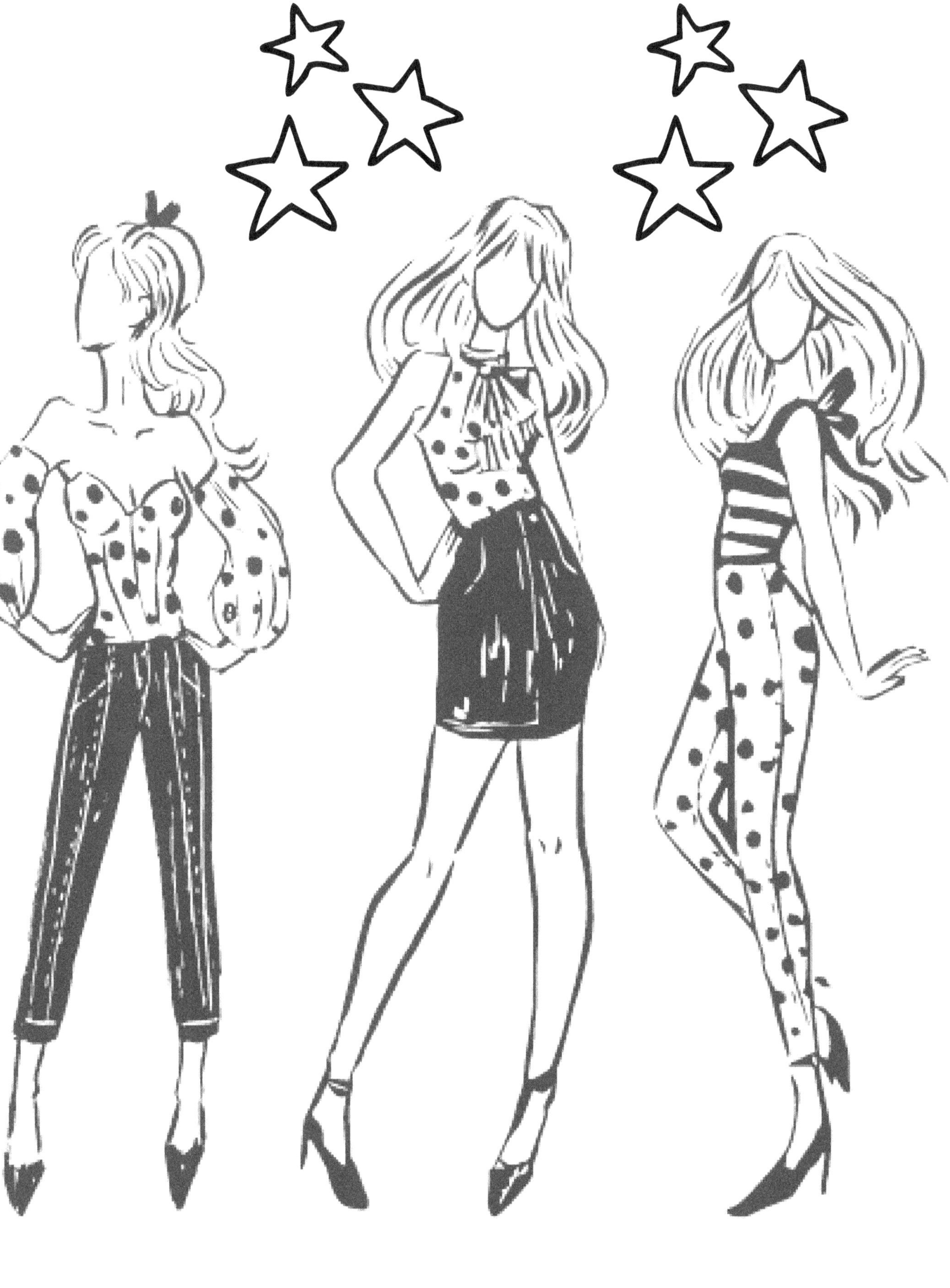

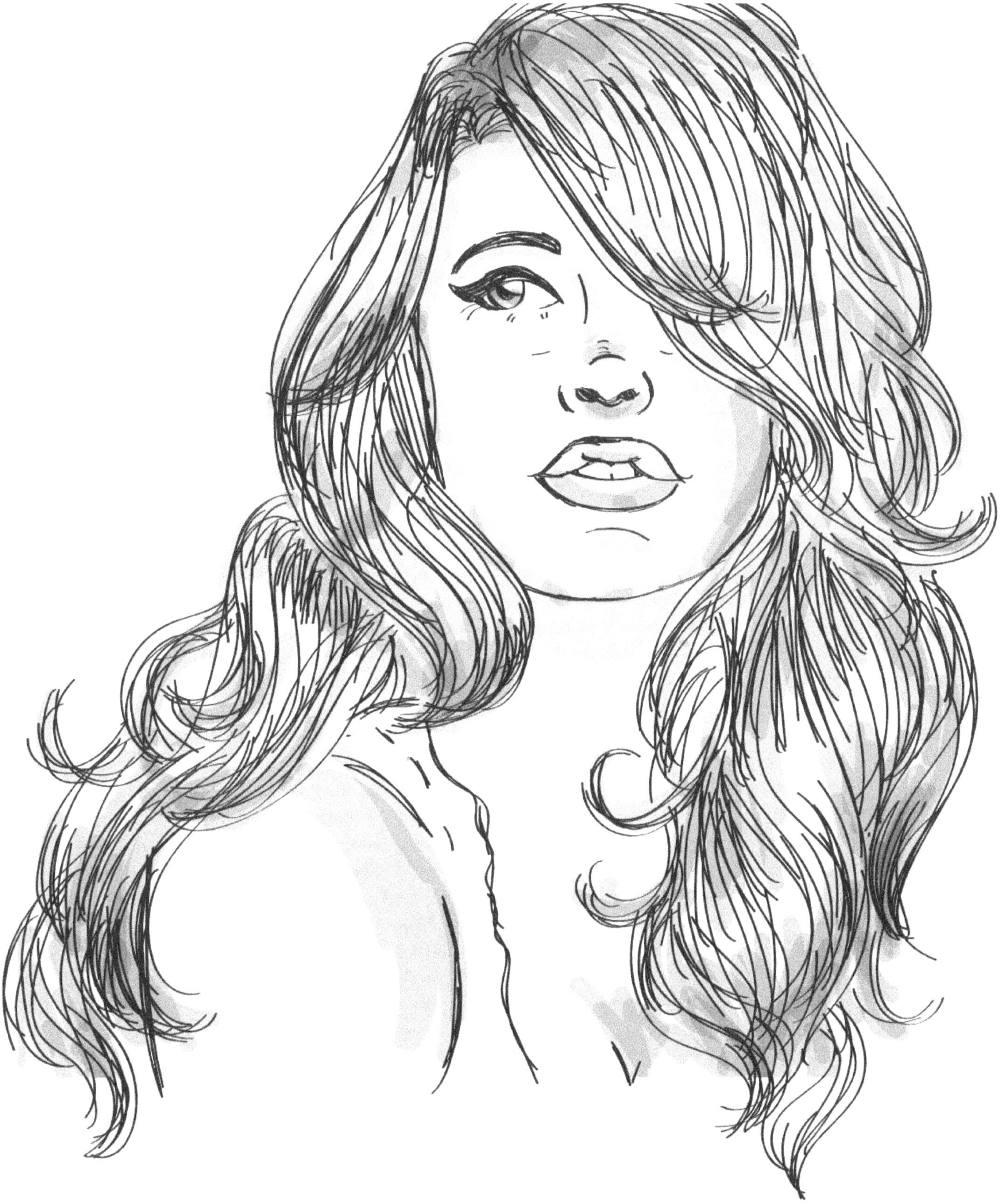

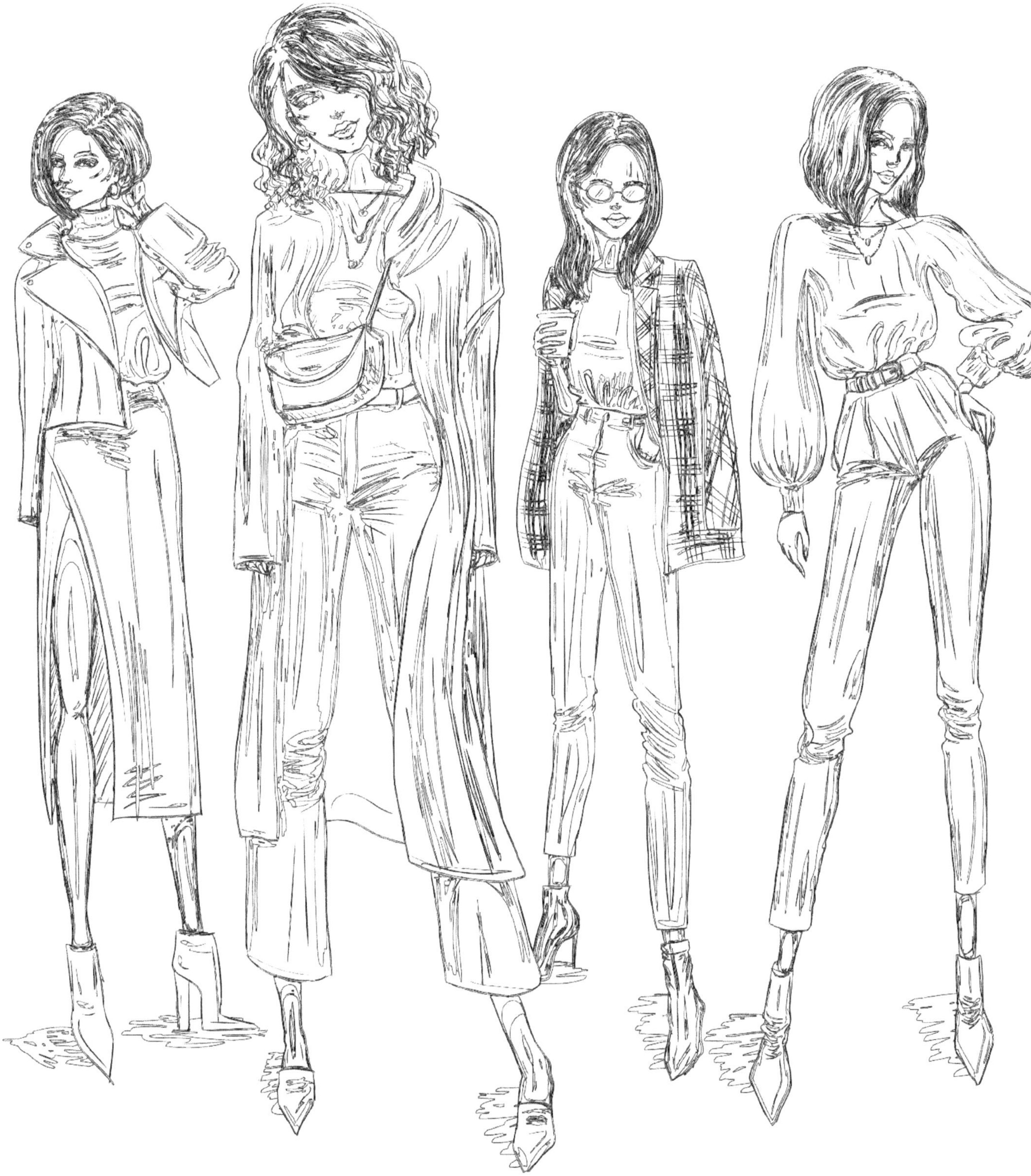

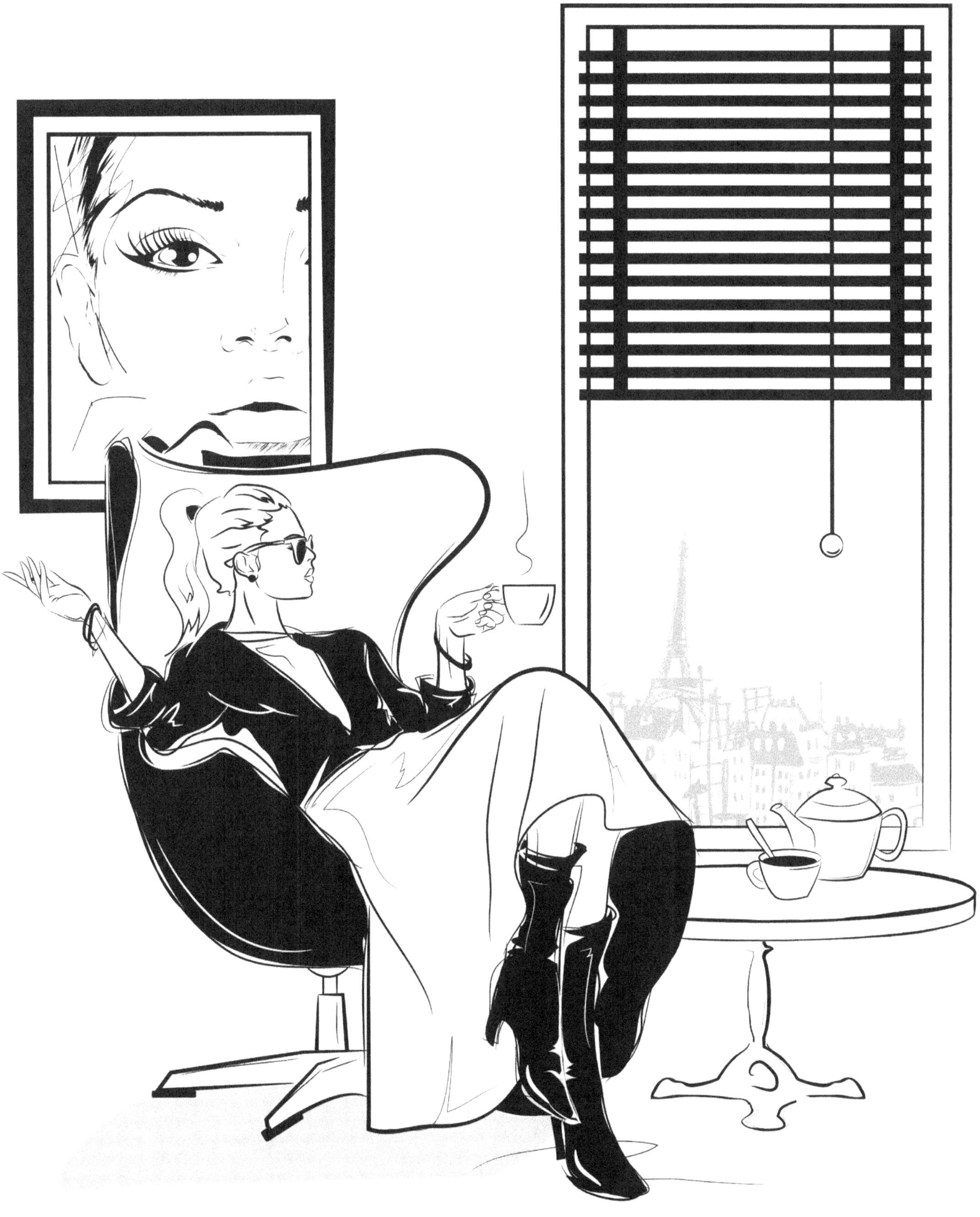

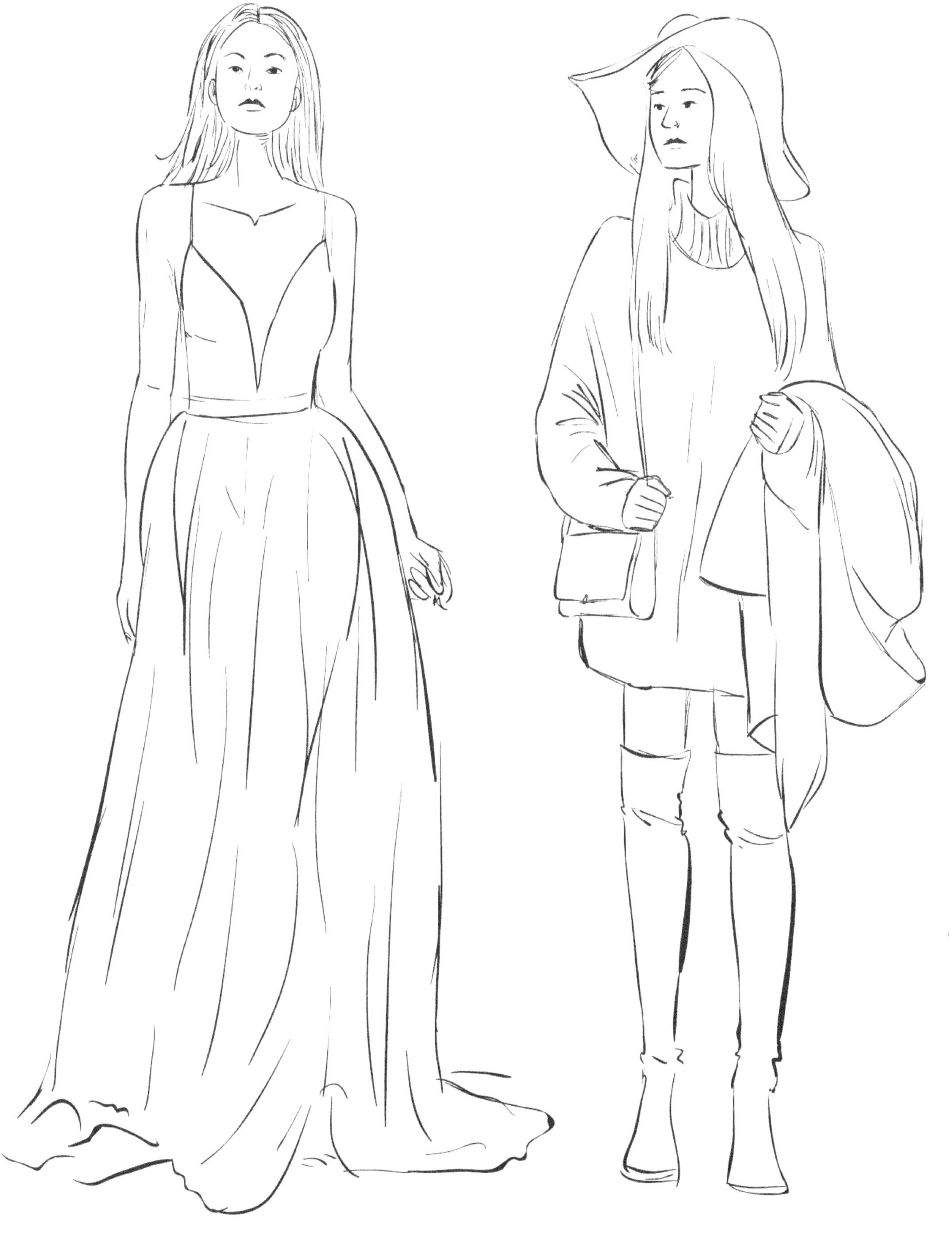

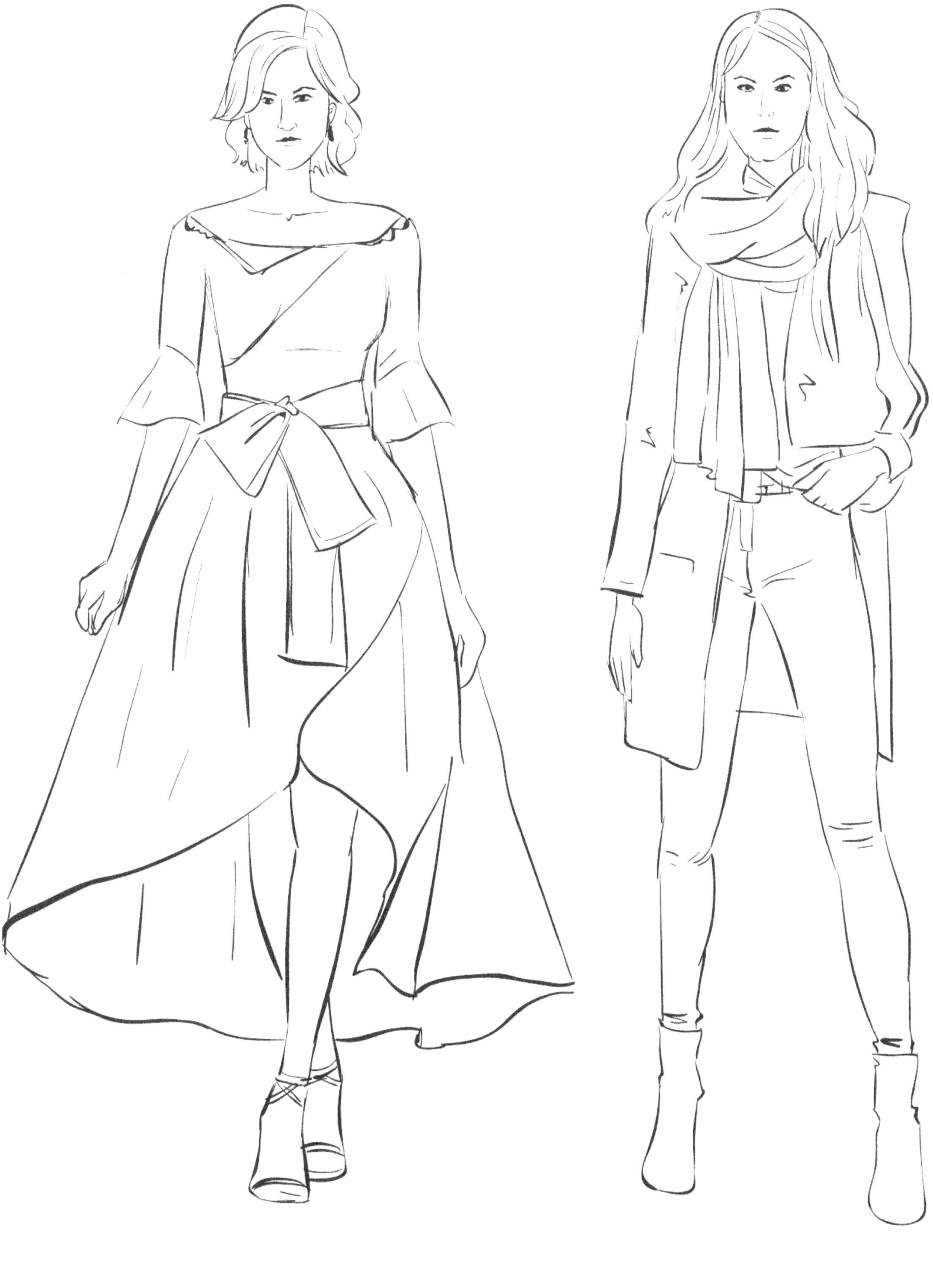

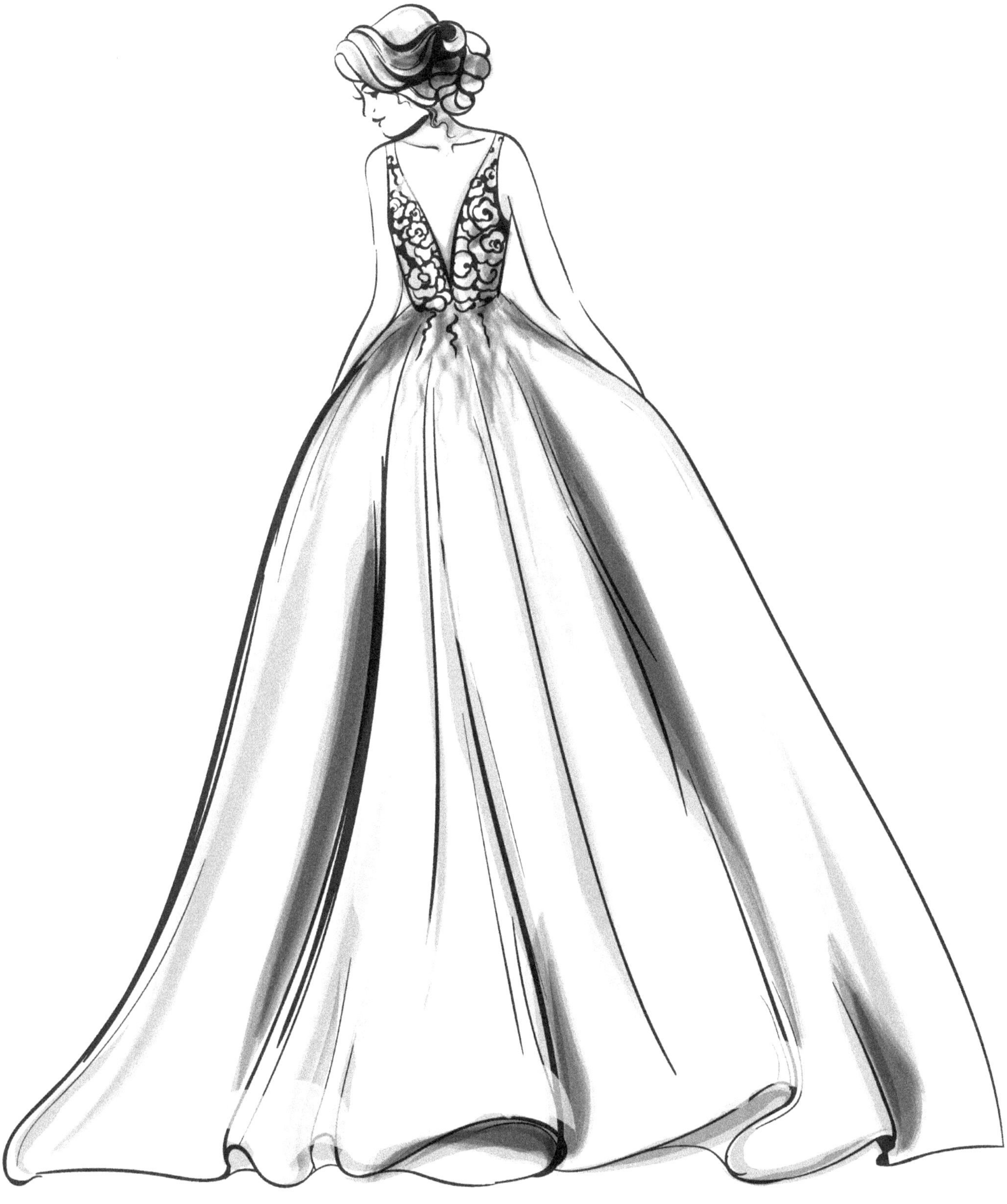

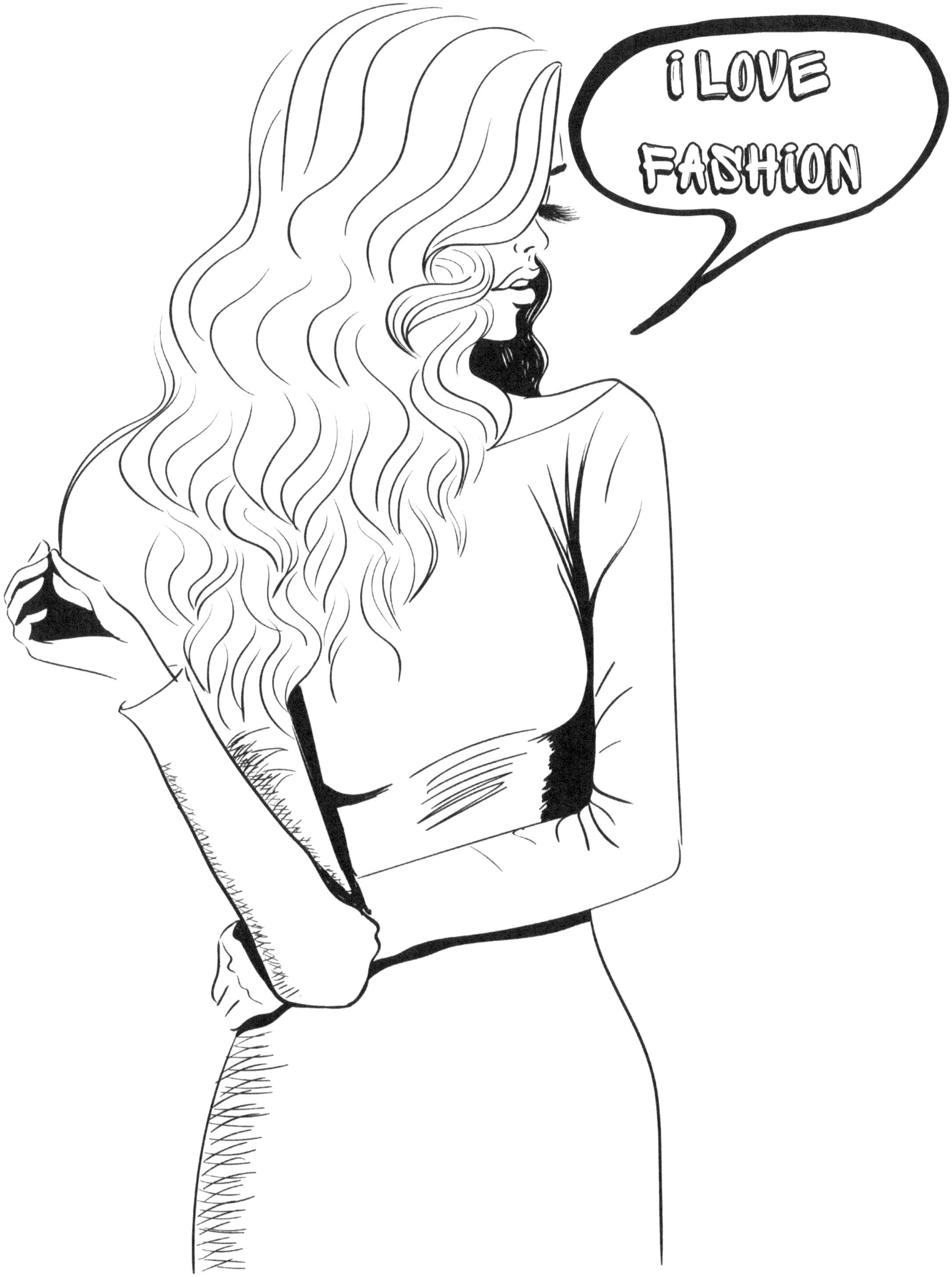
i LOVE FASHiON

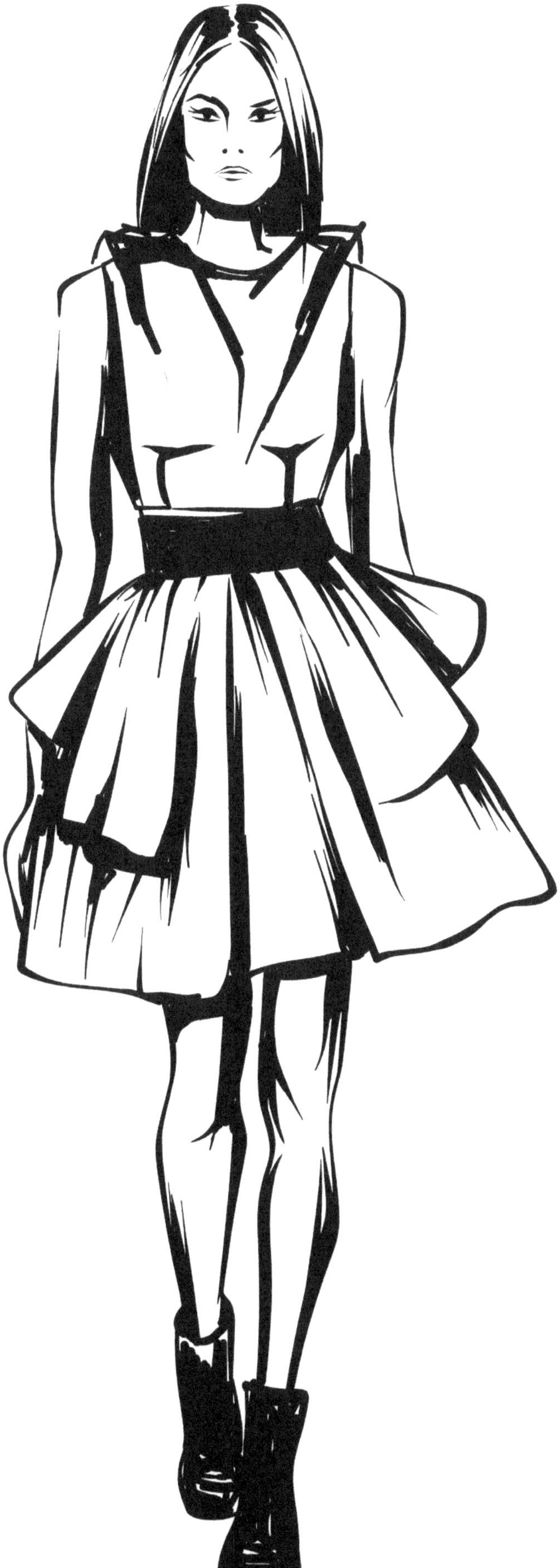

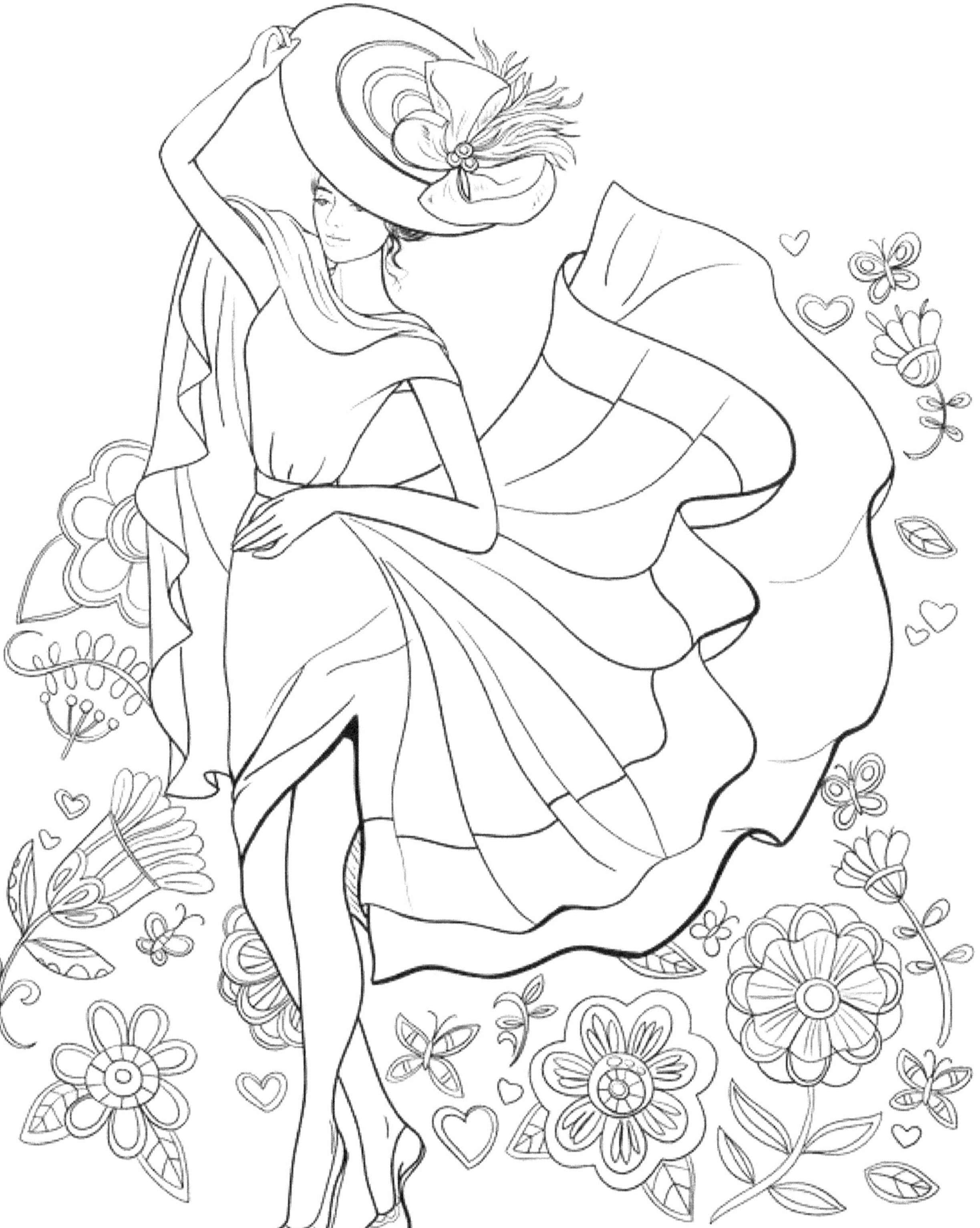

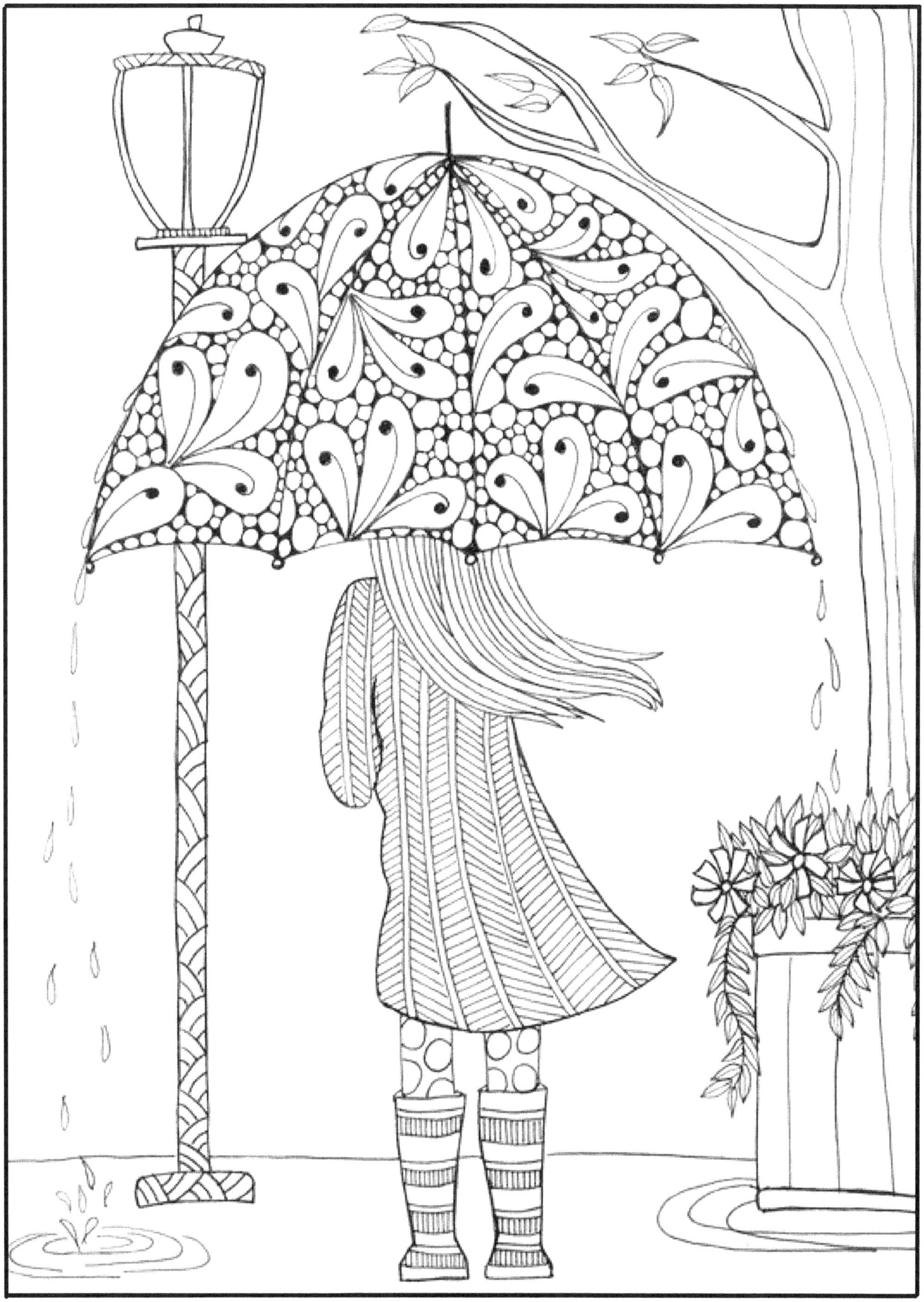

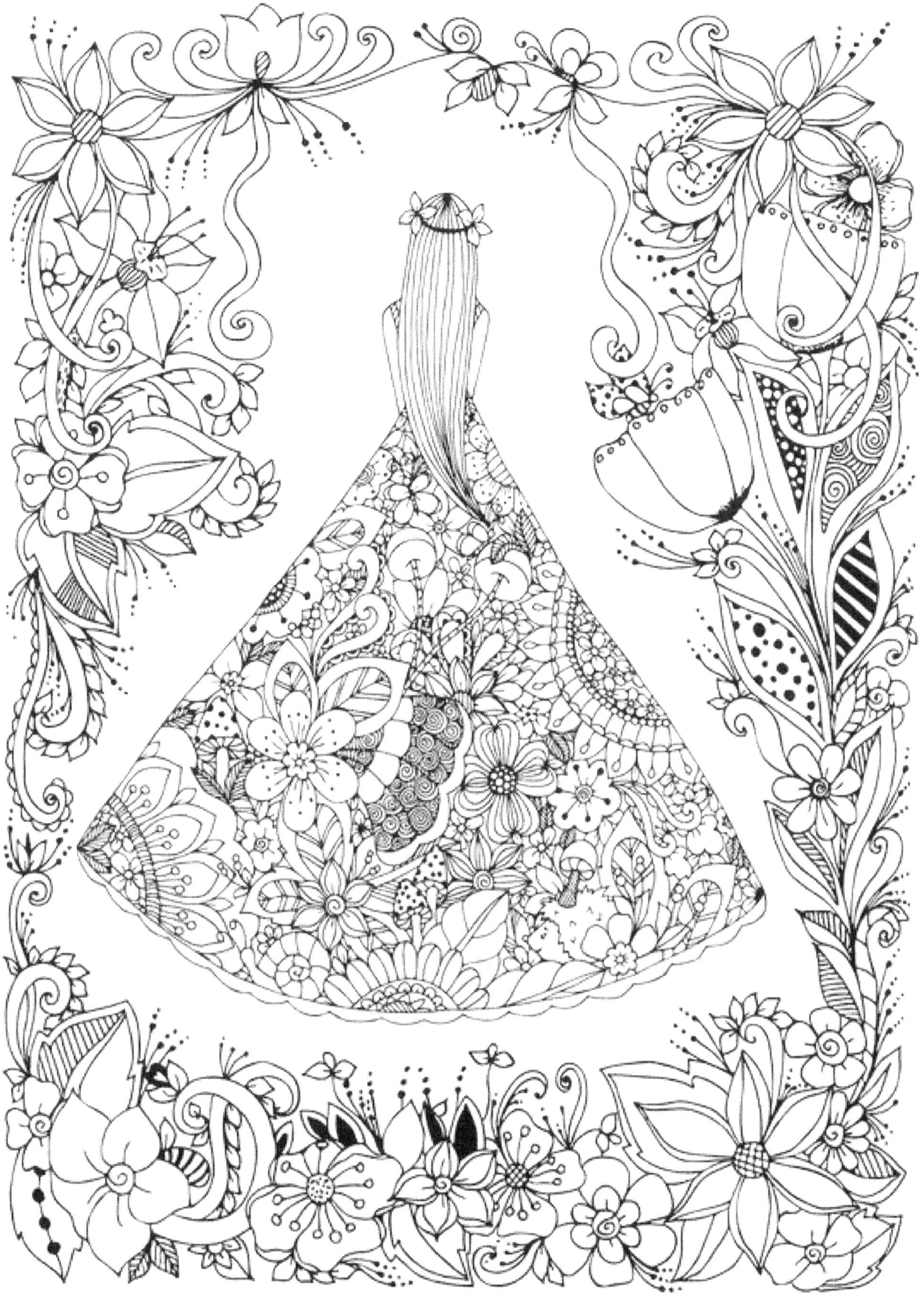

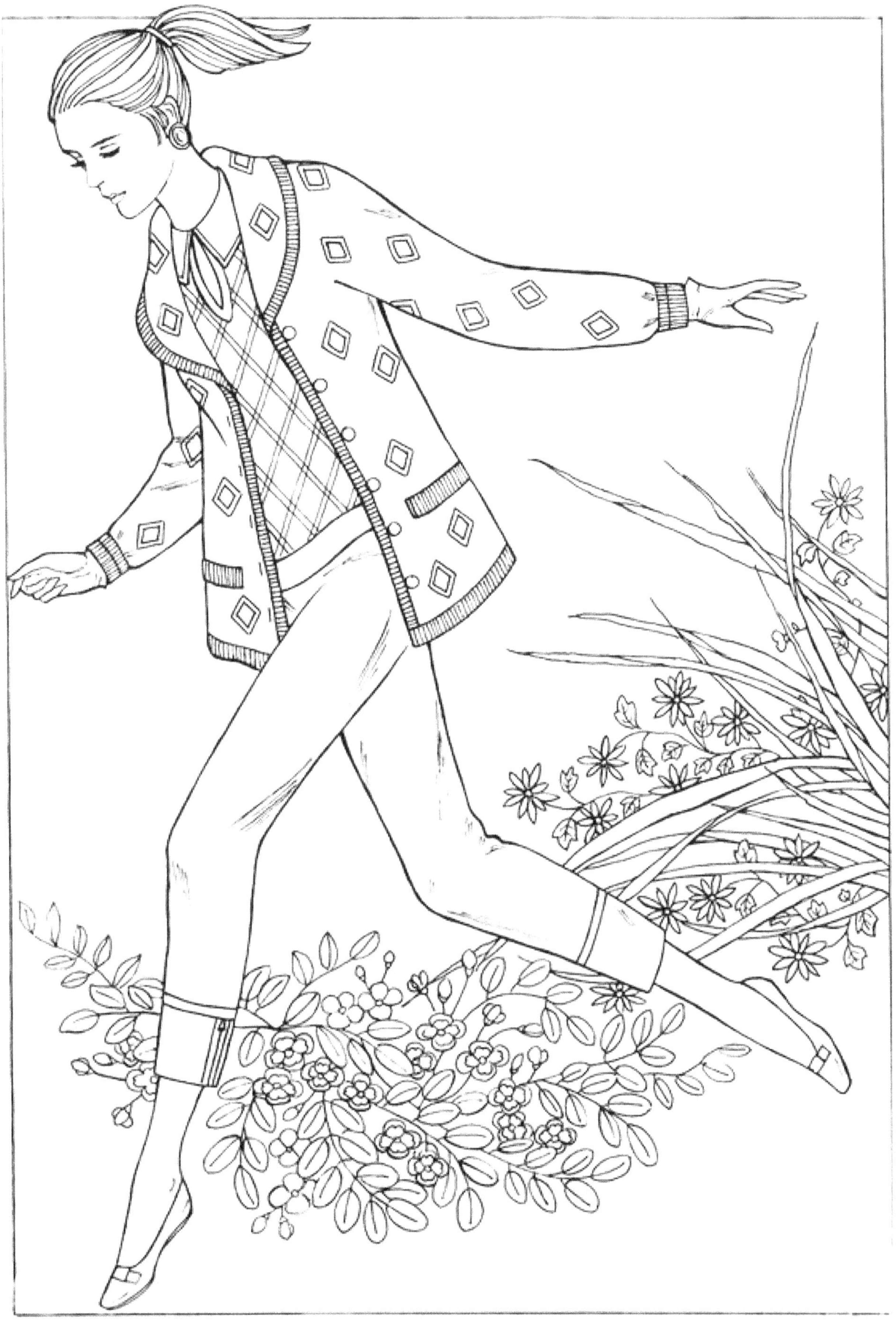

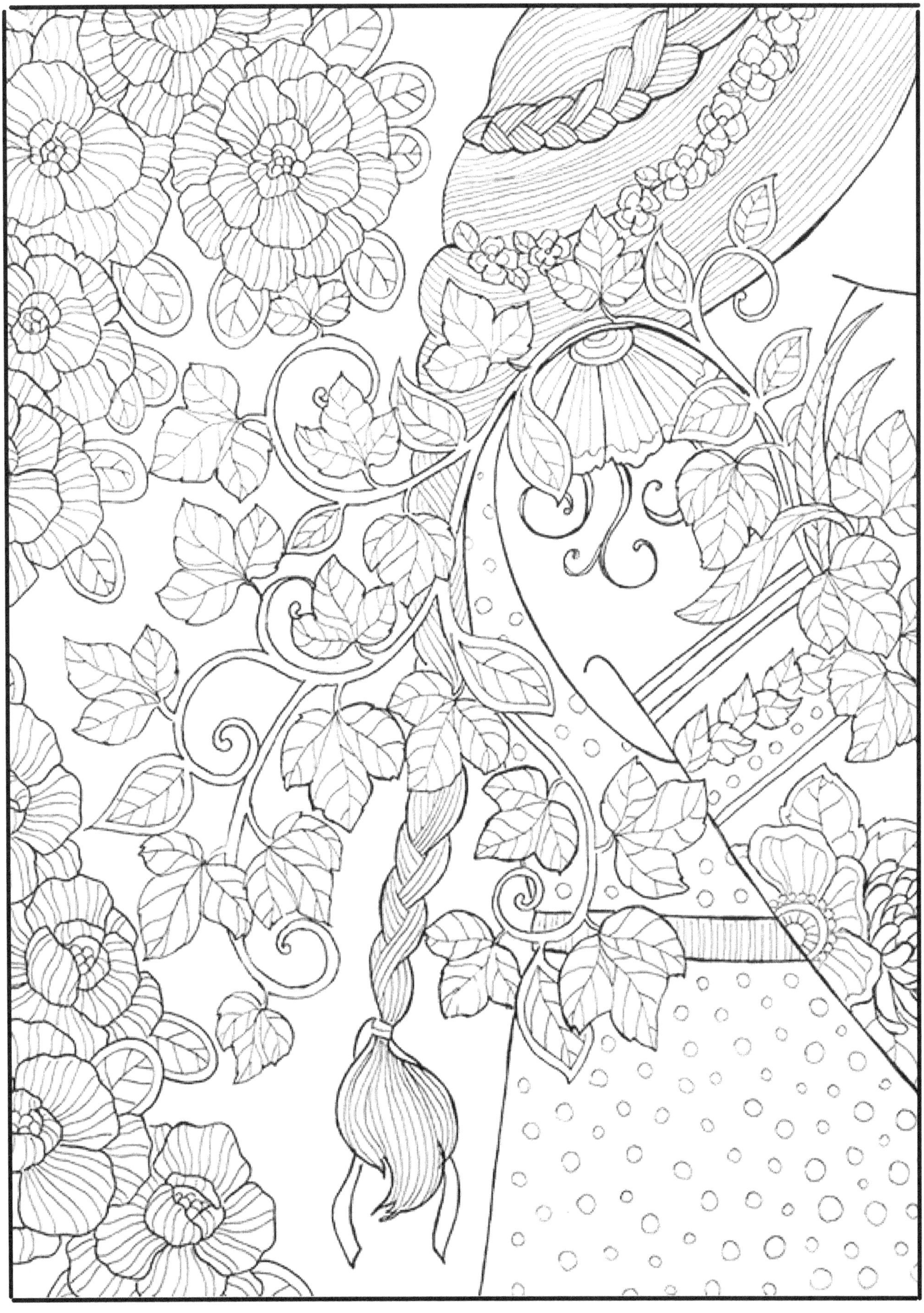

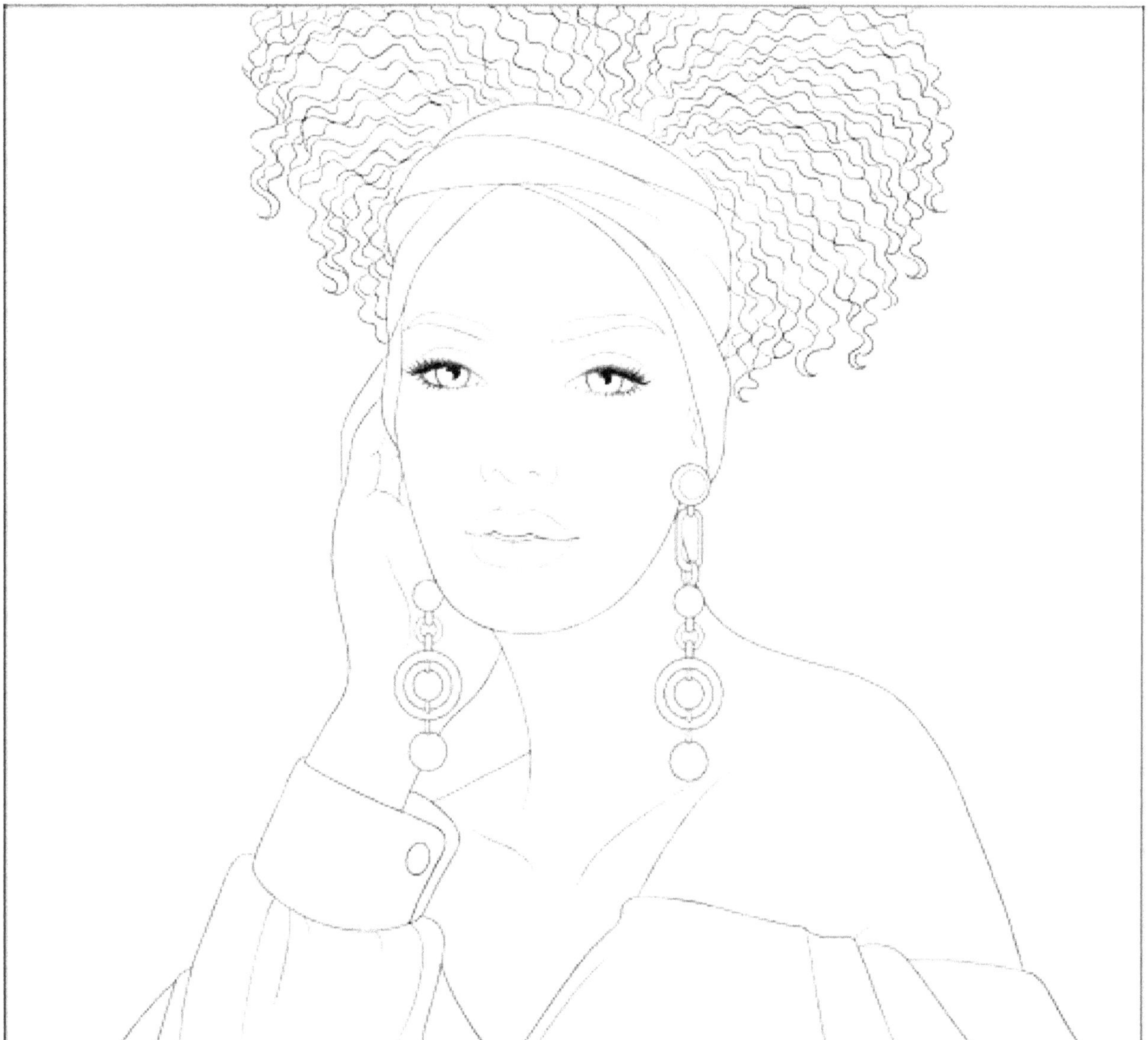

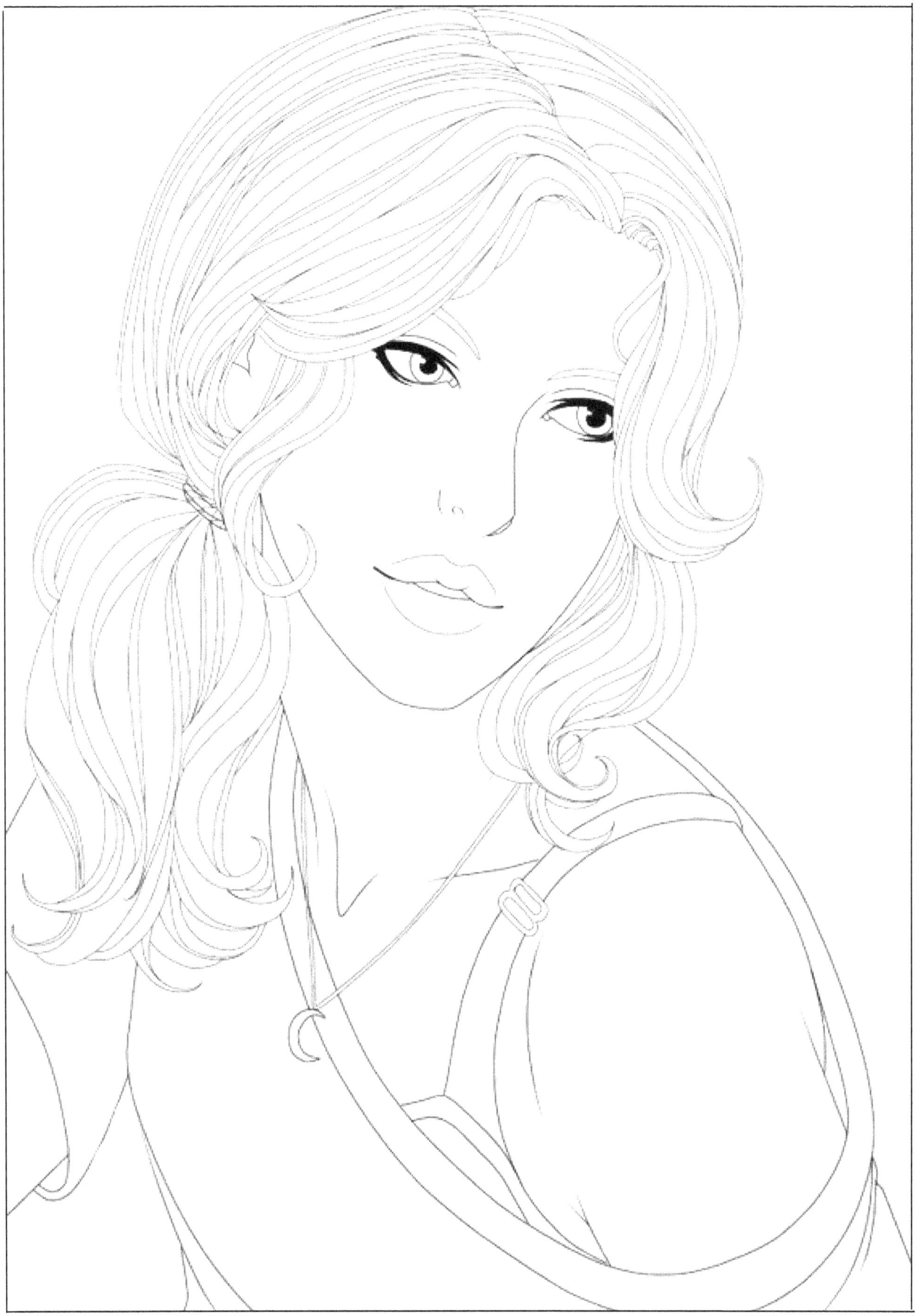

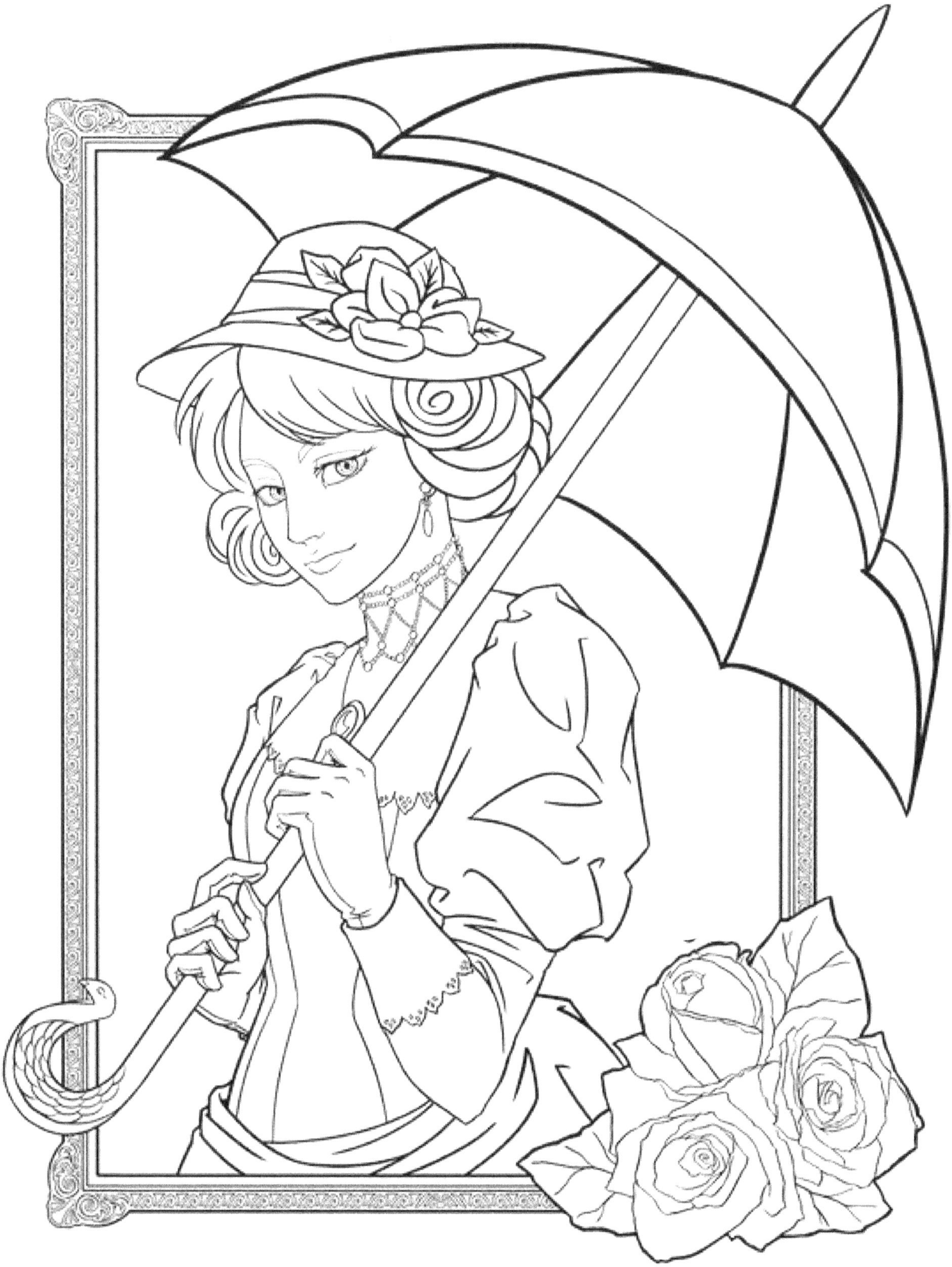

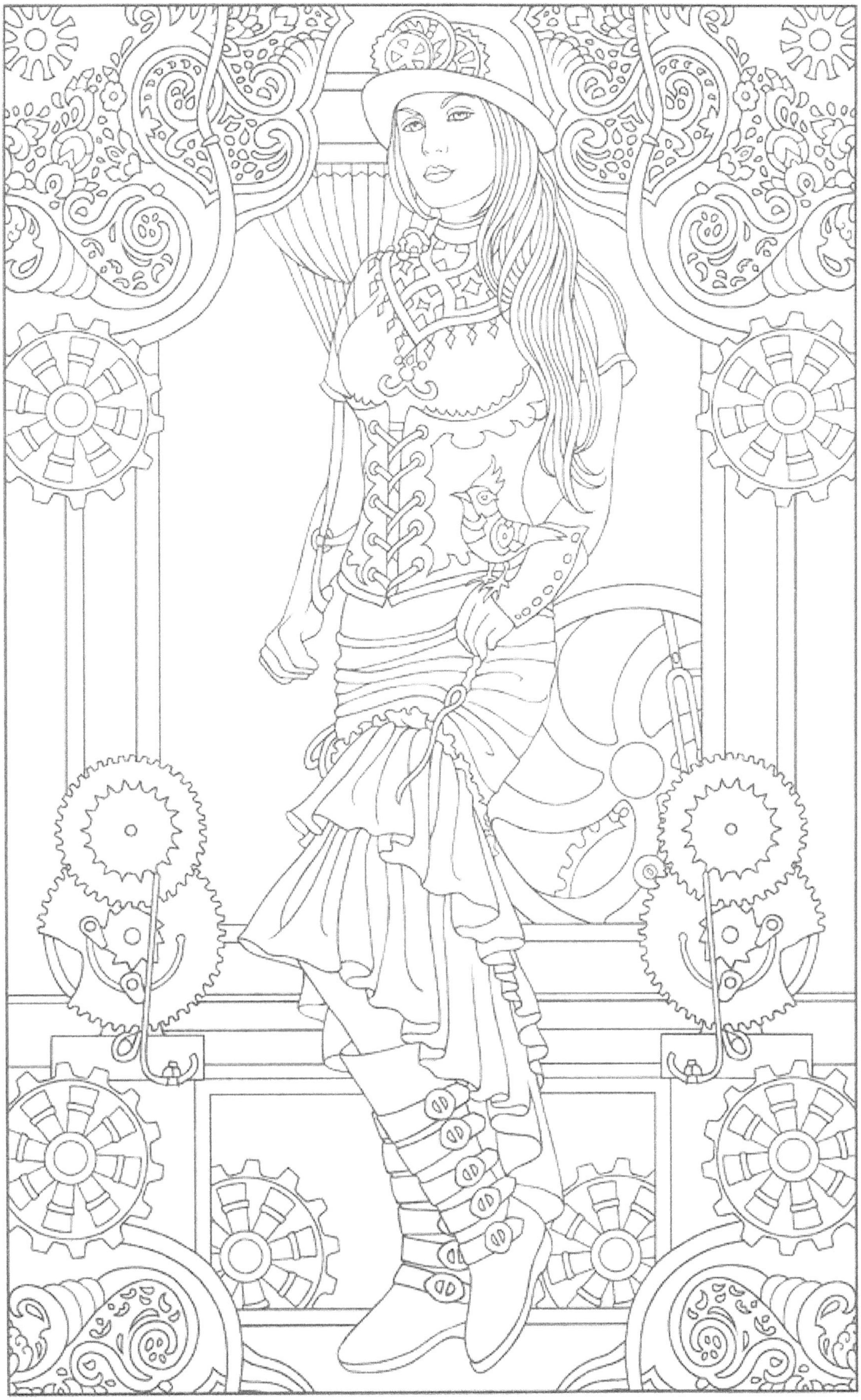

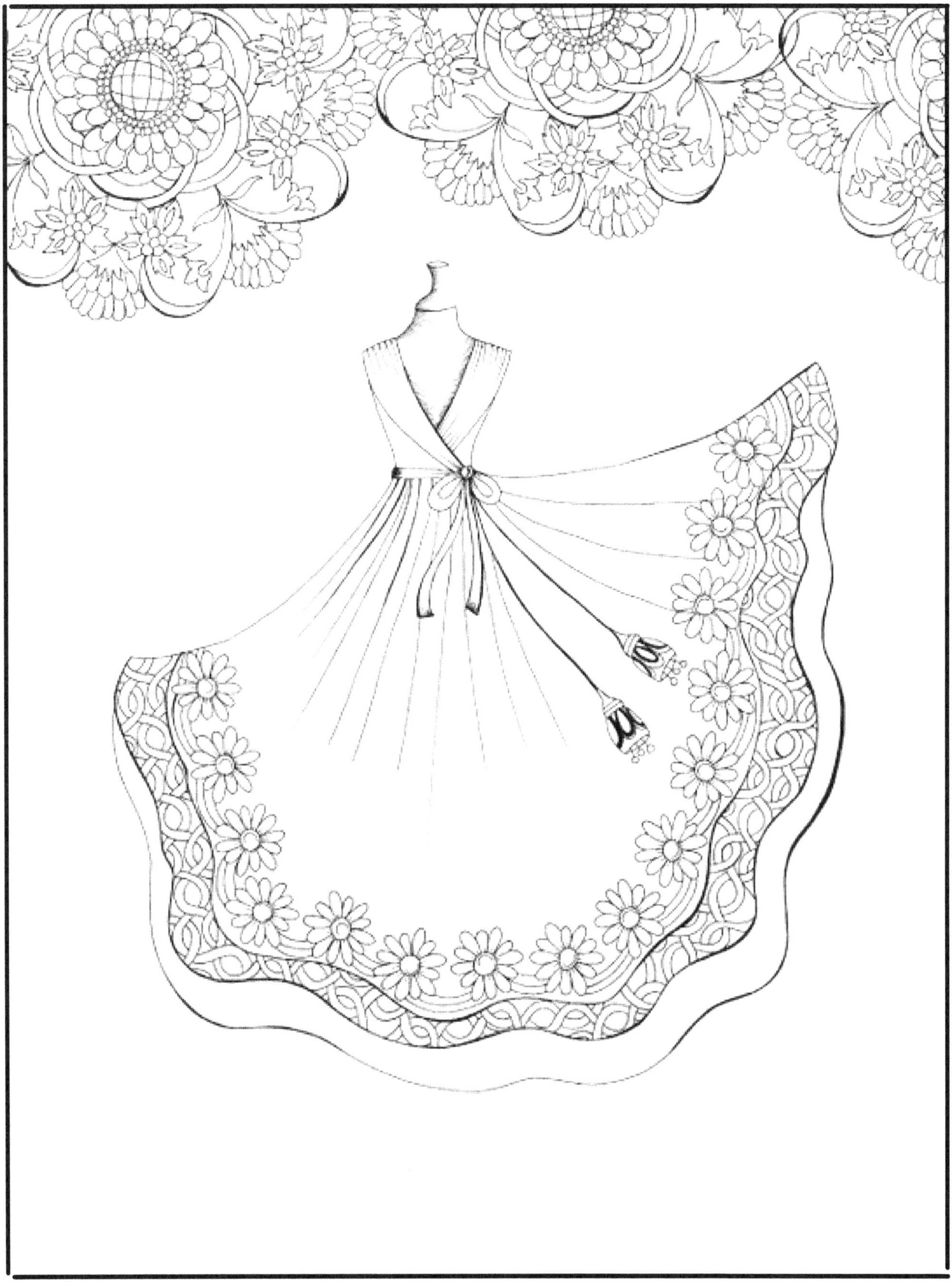

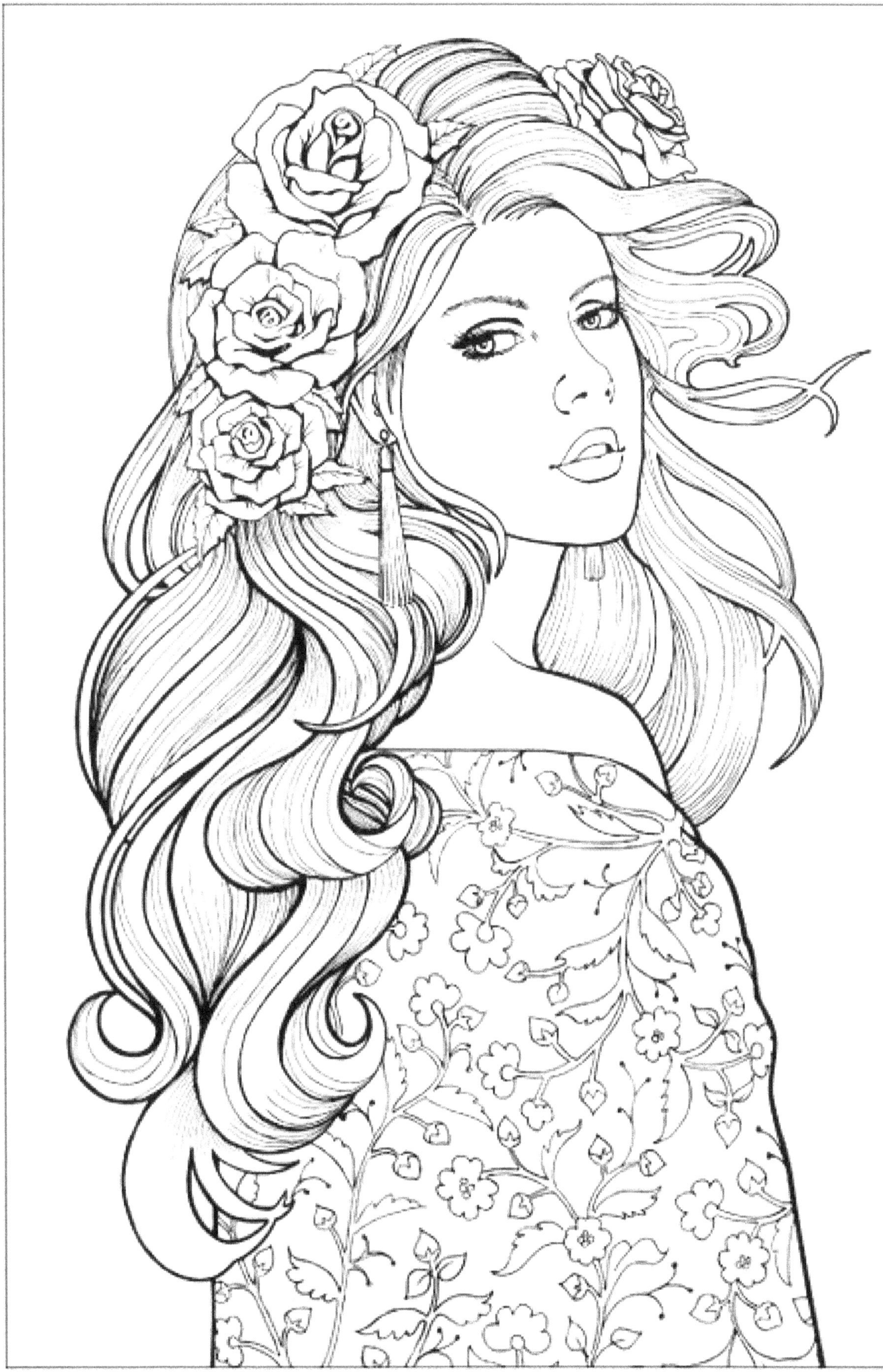

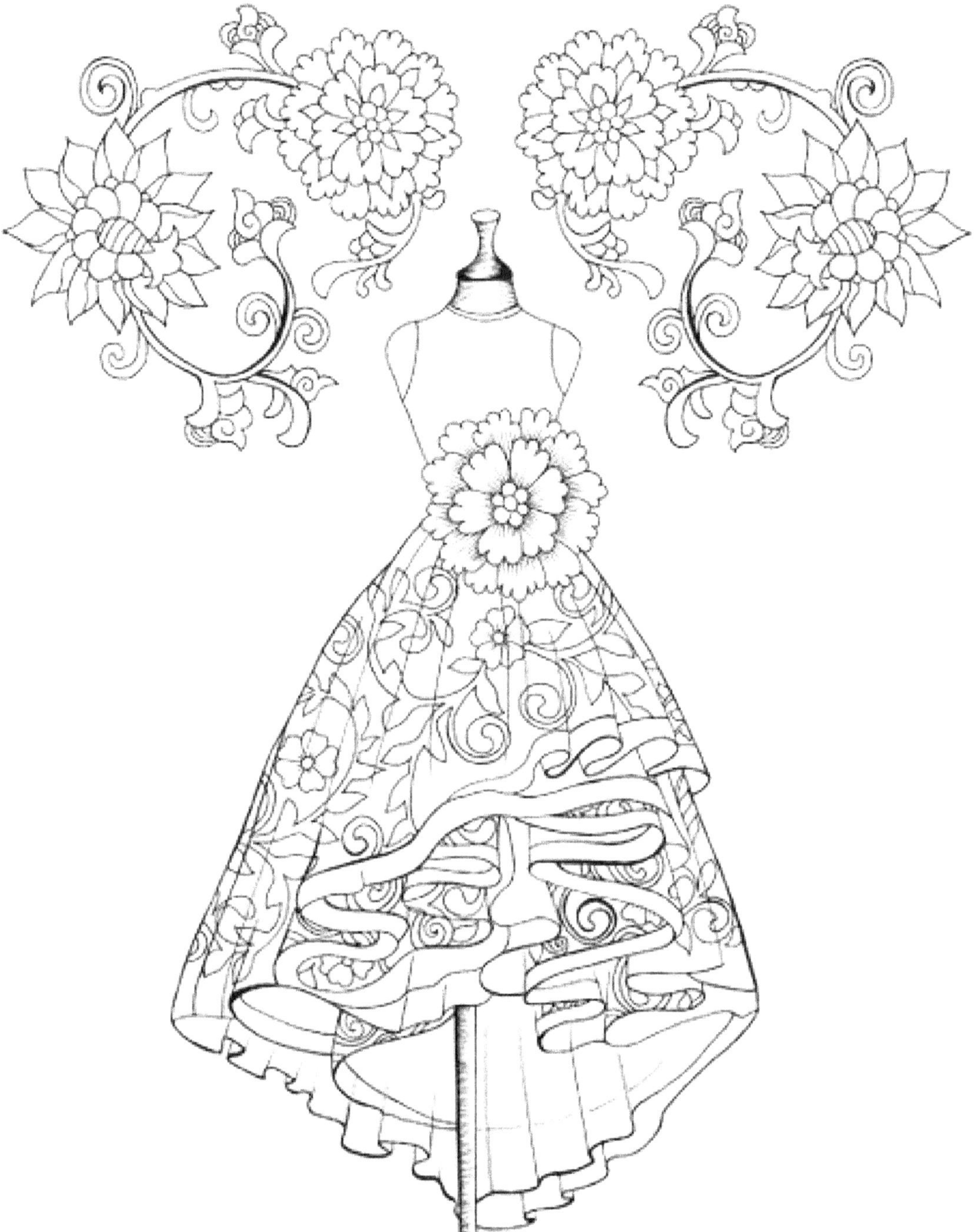

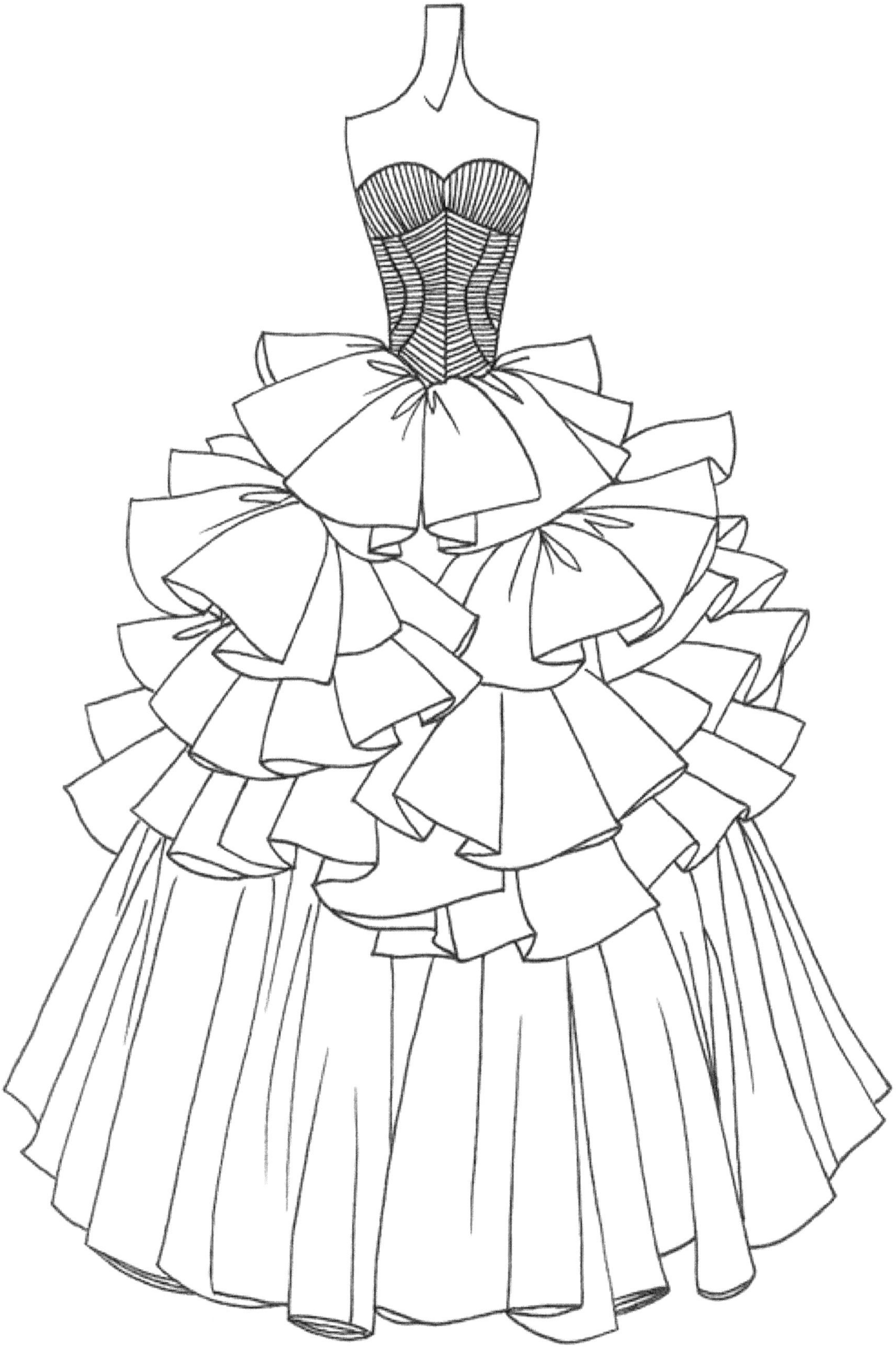

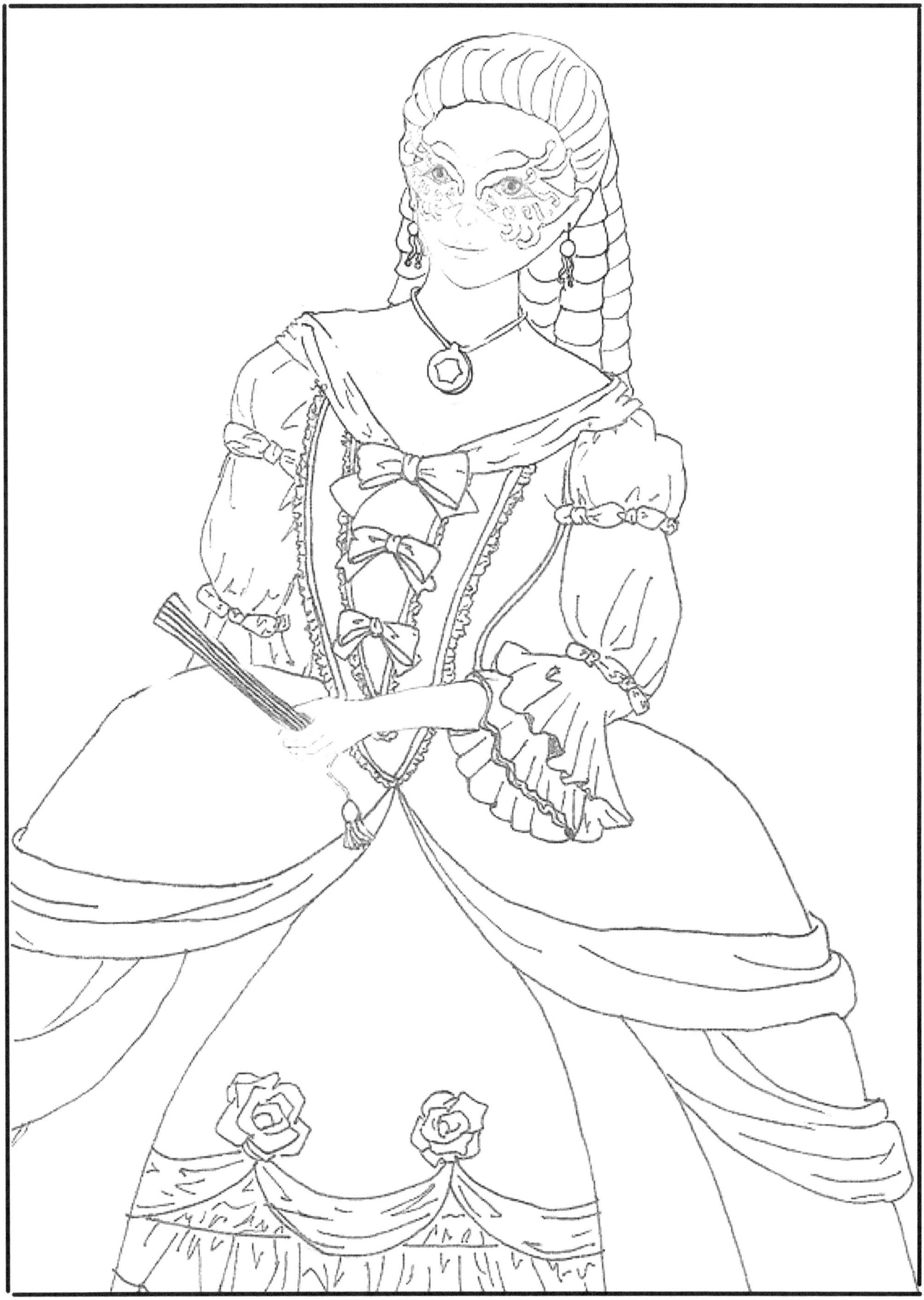

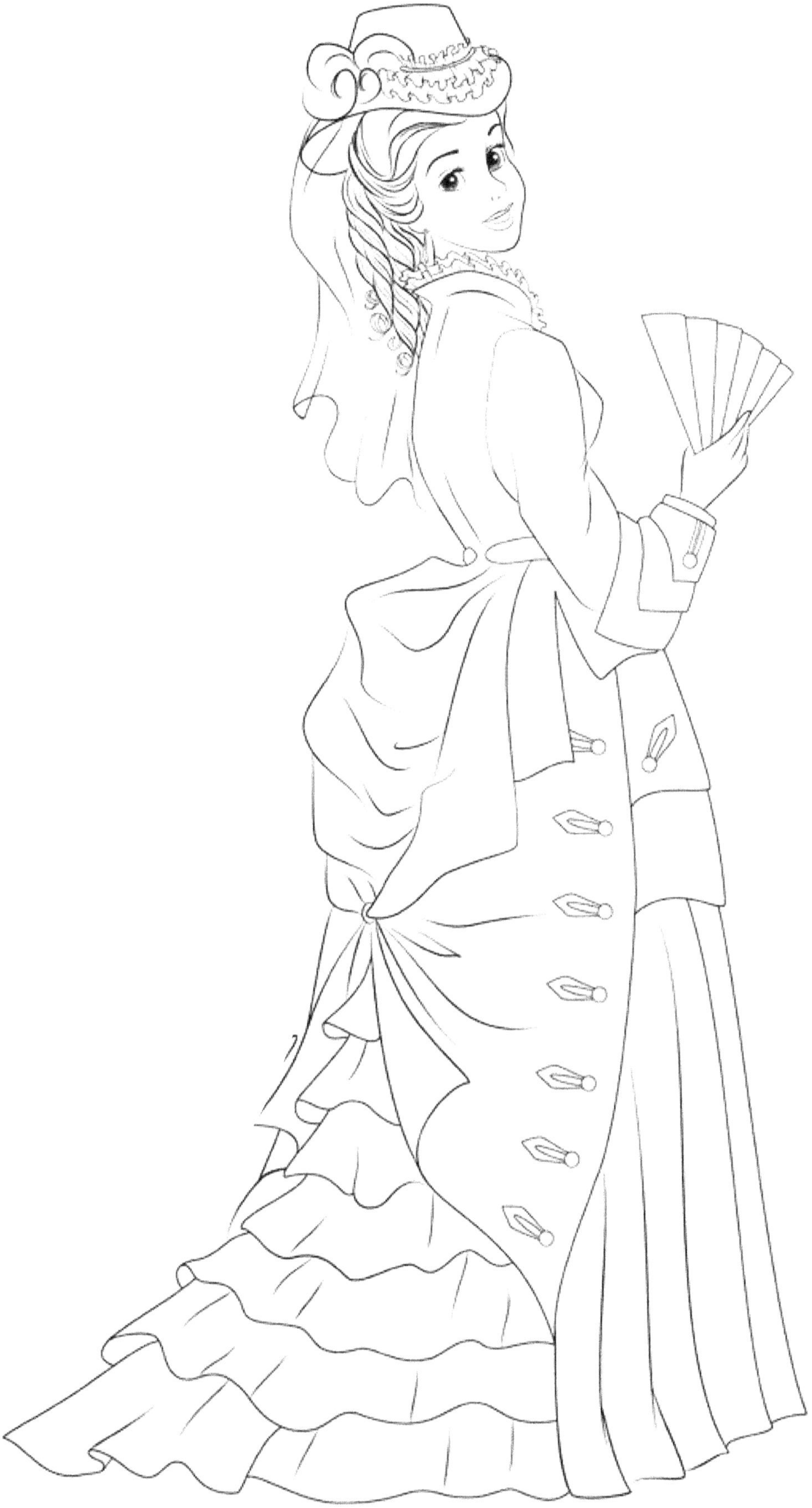

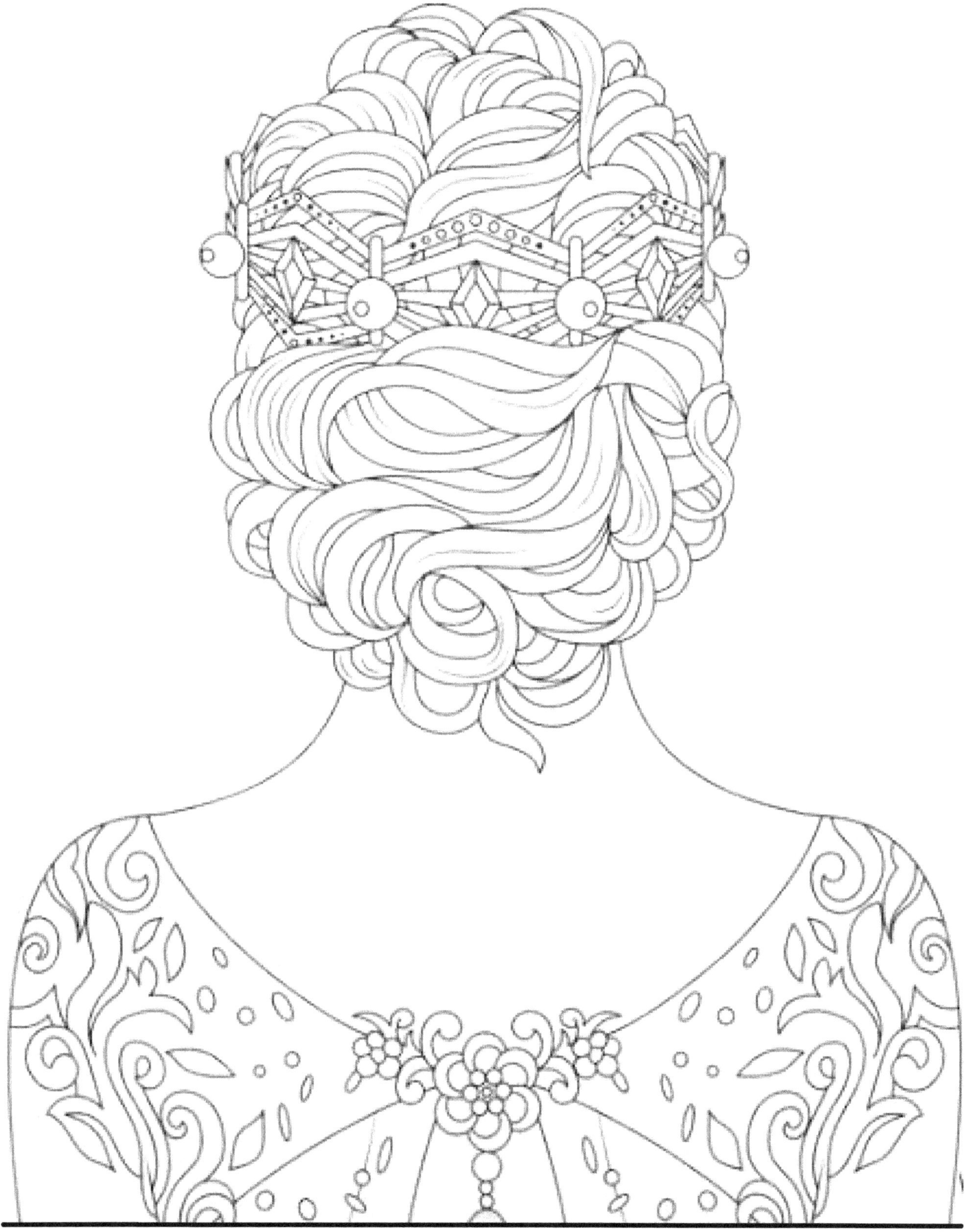

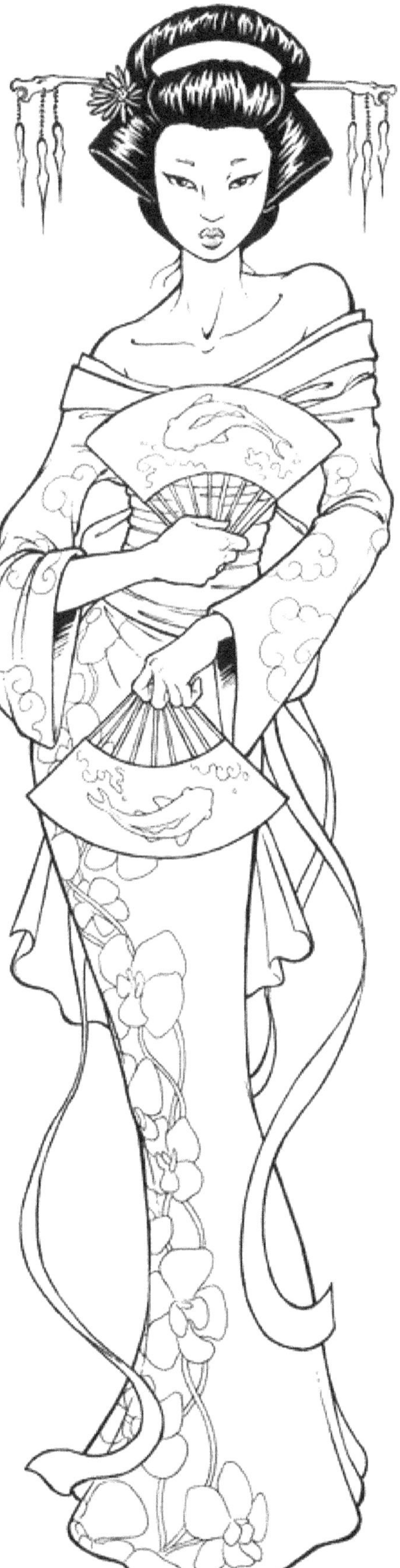

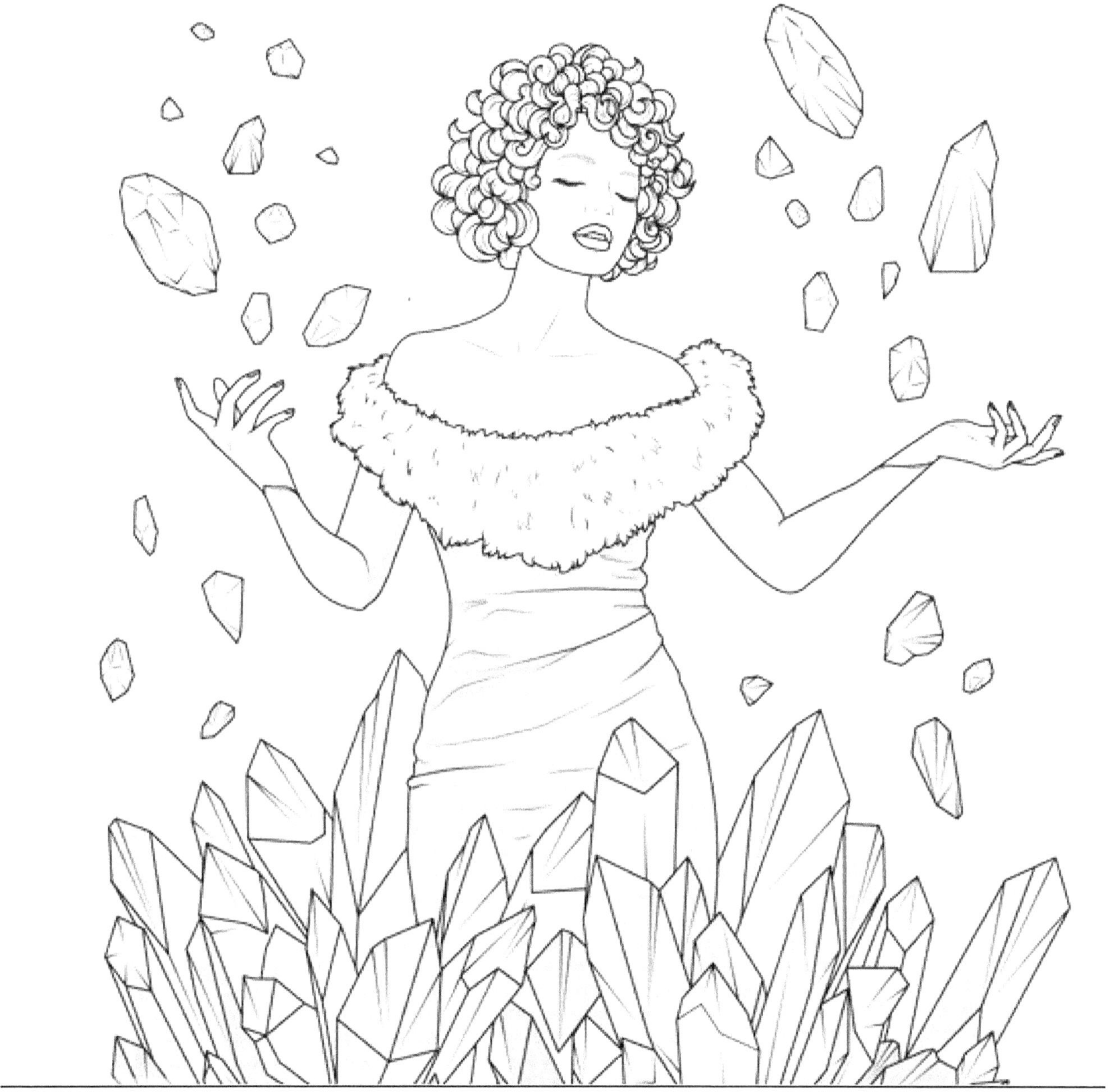

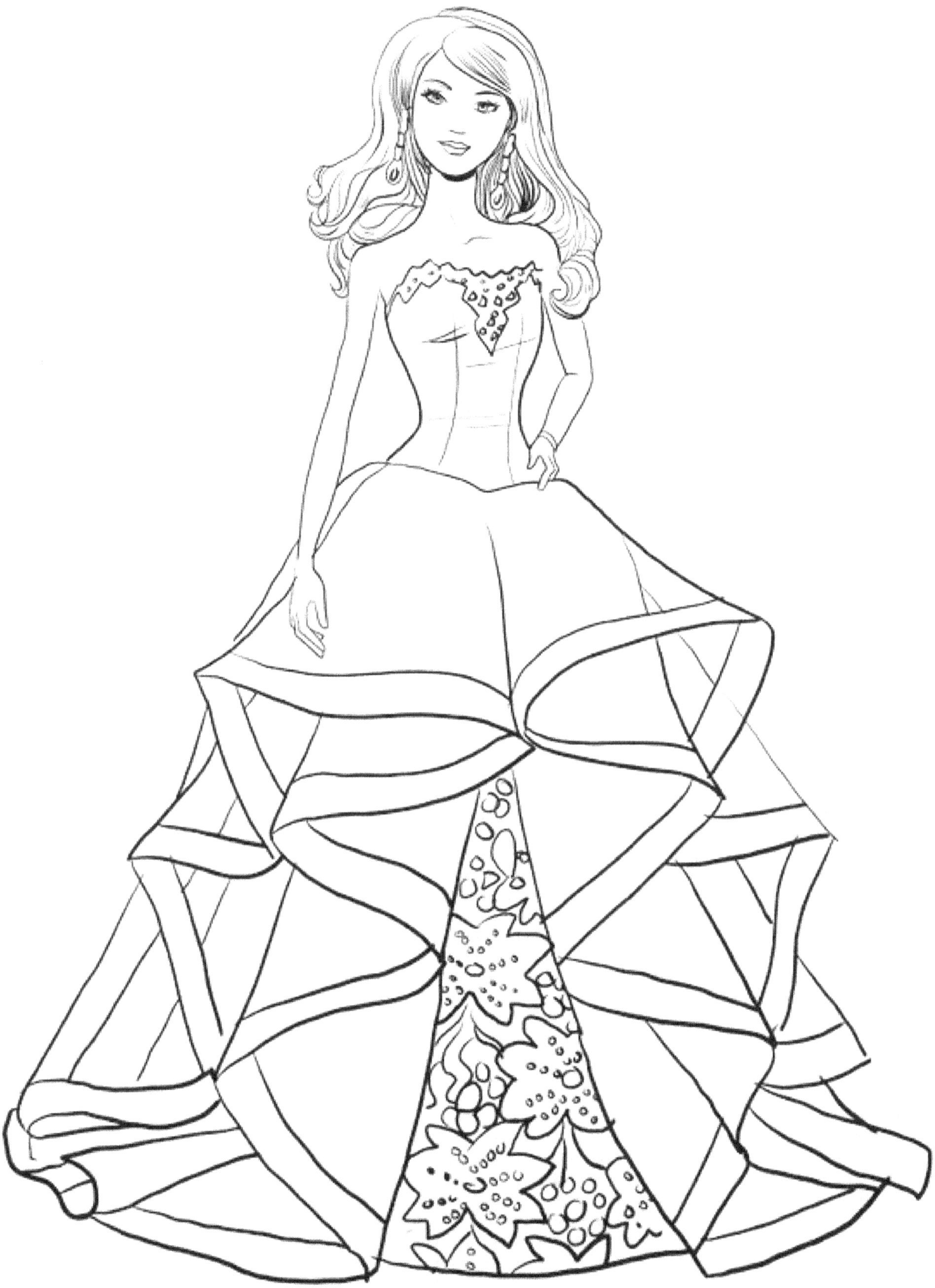

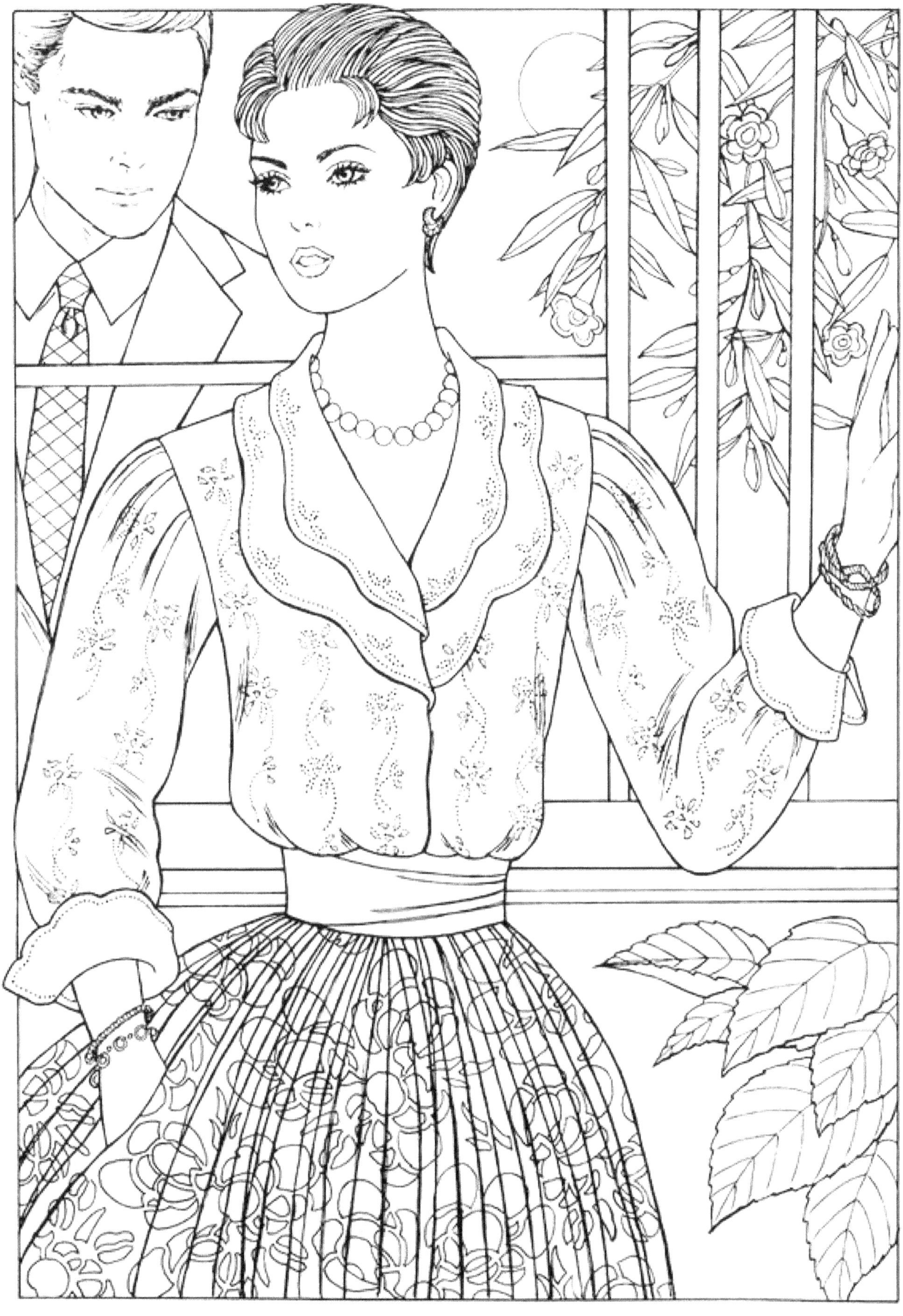

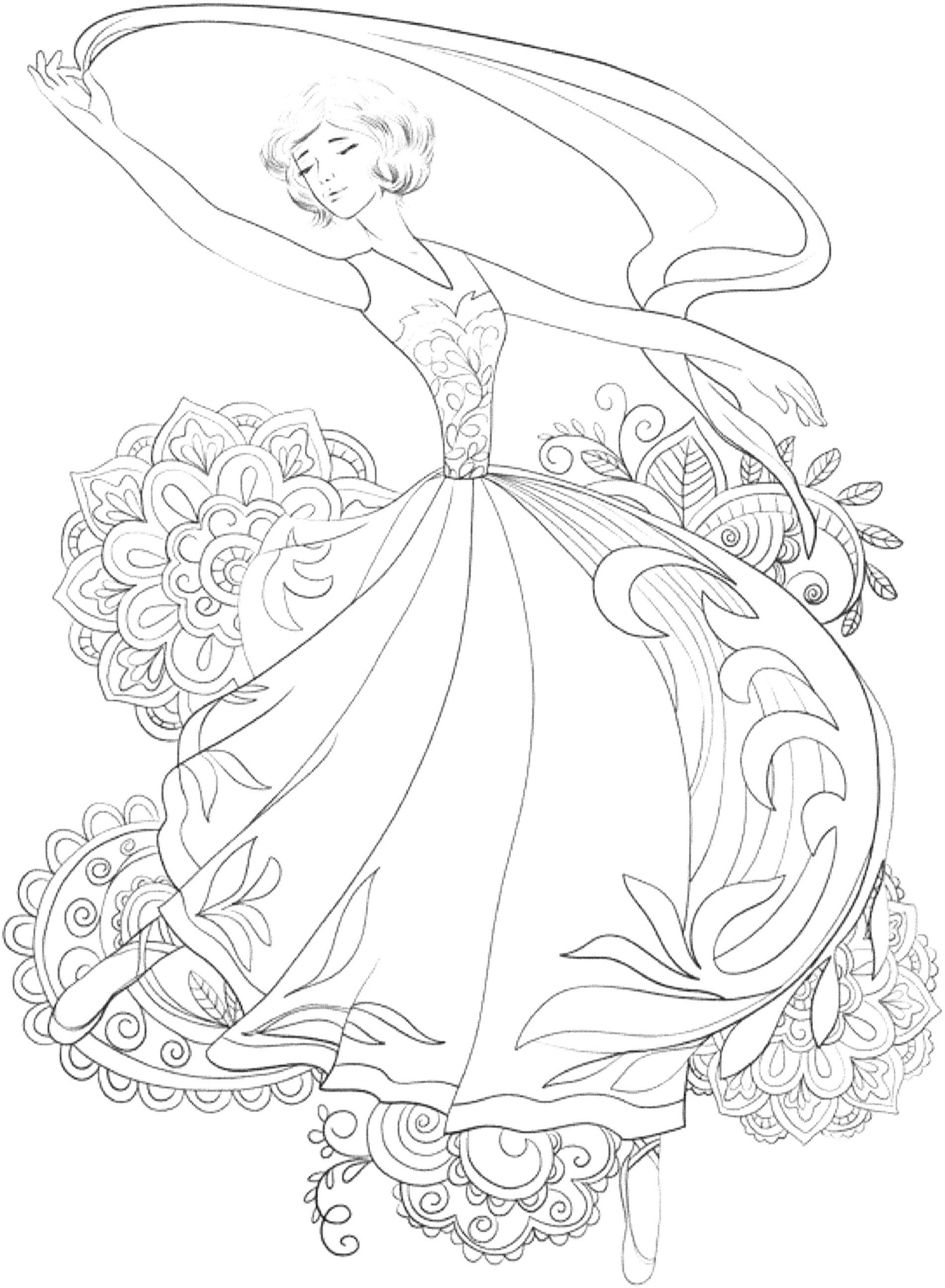

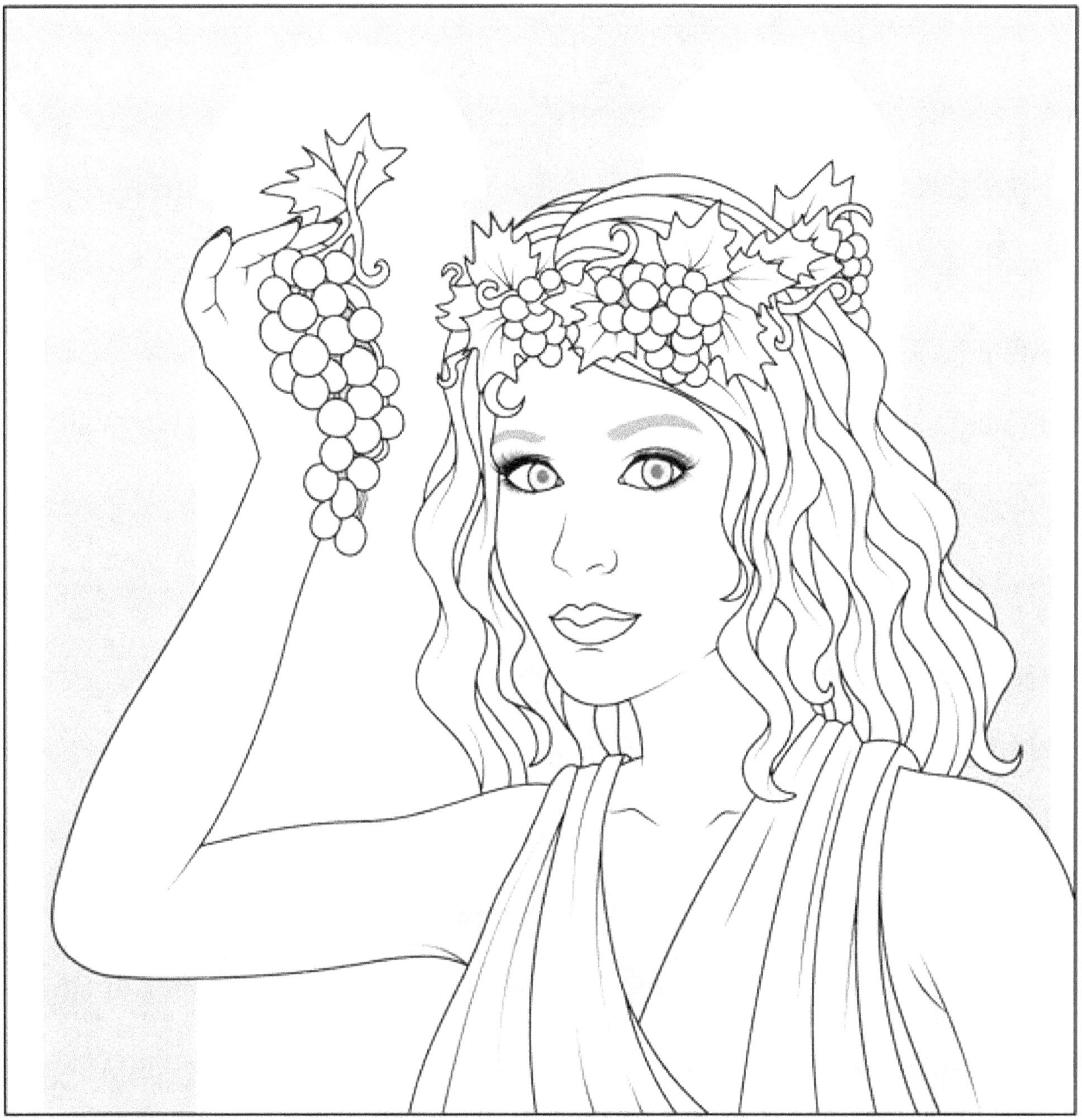

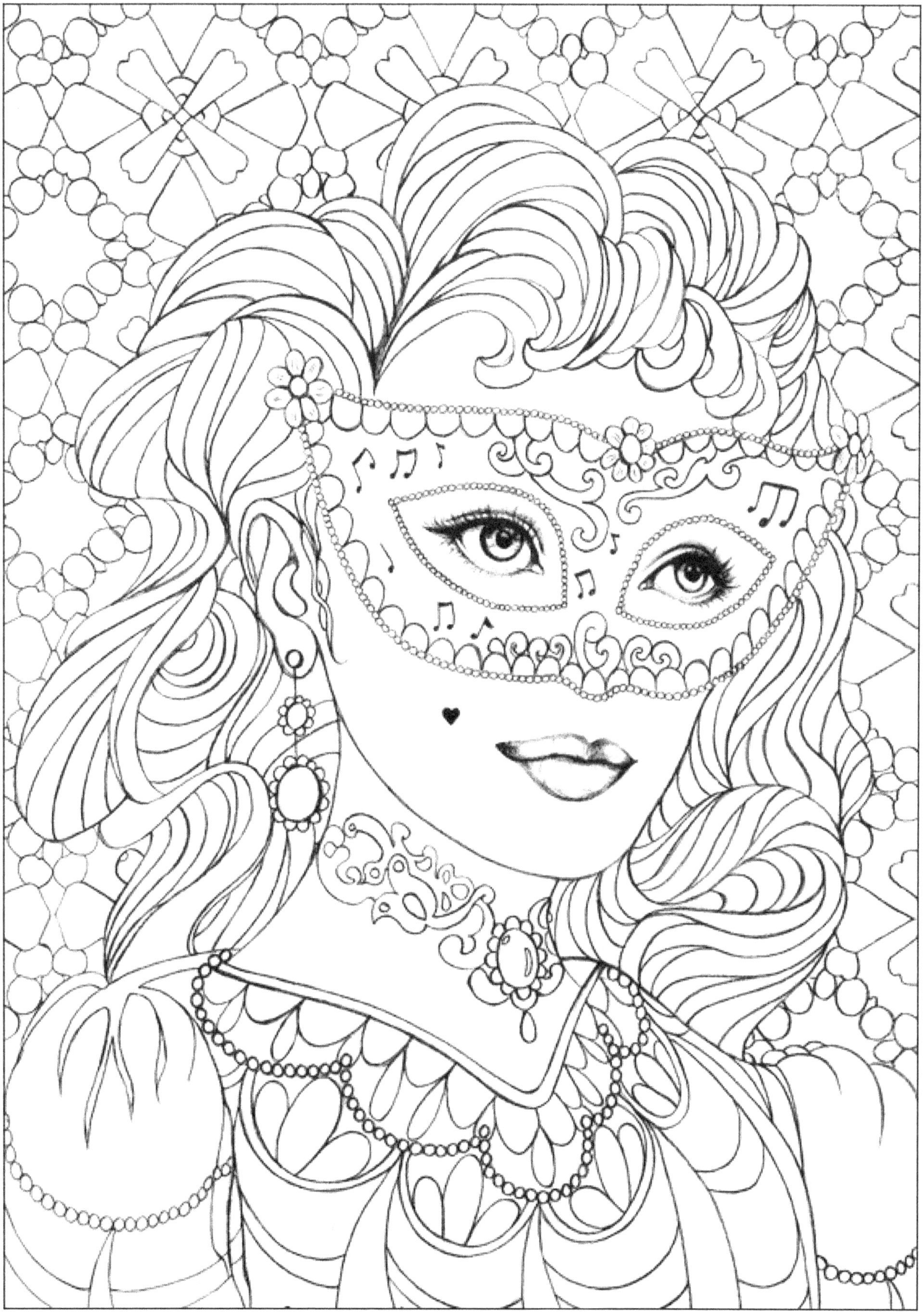

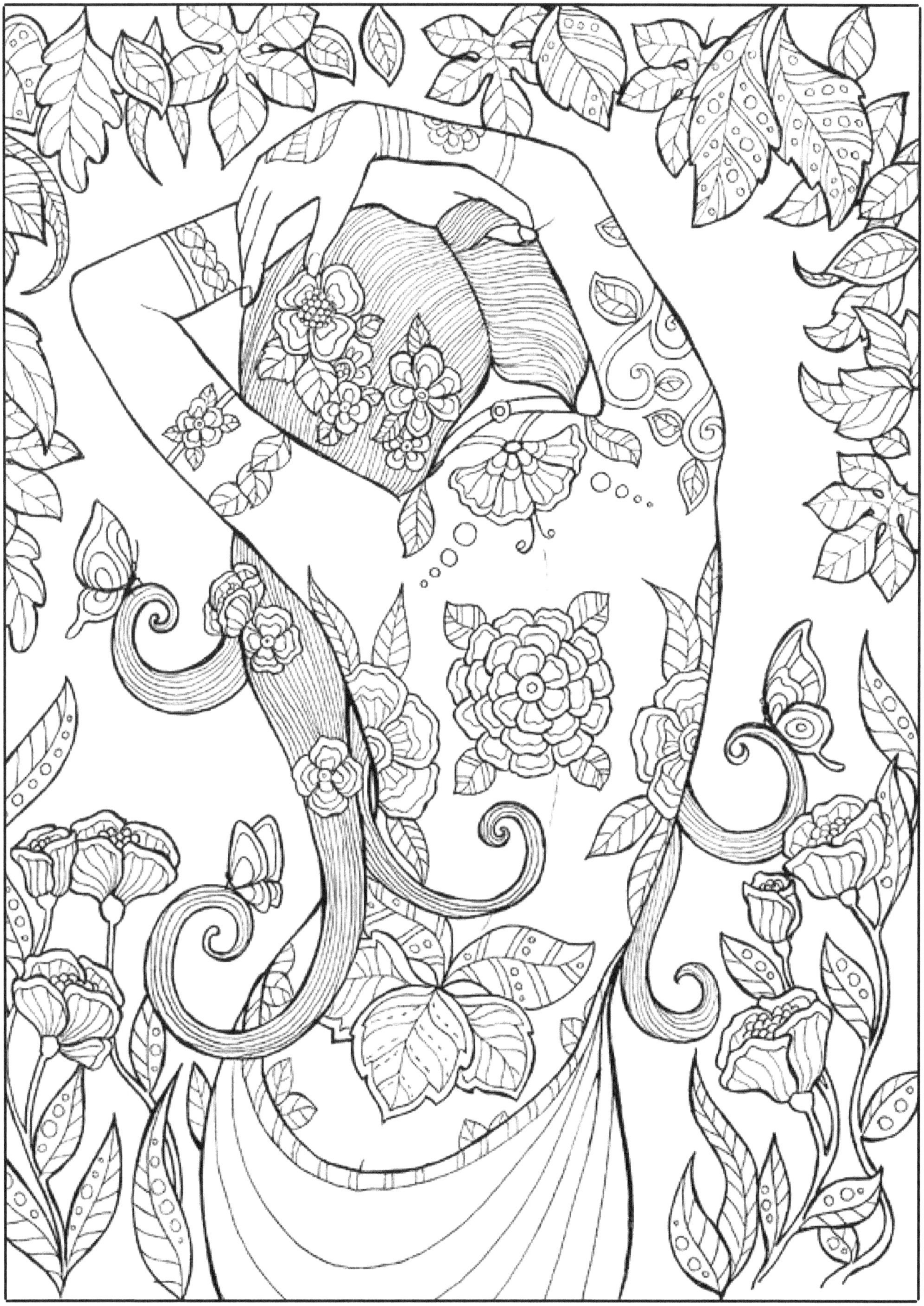

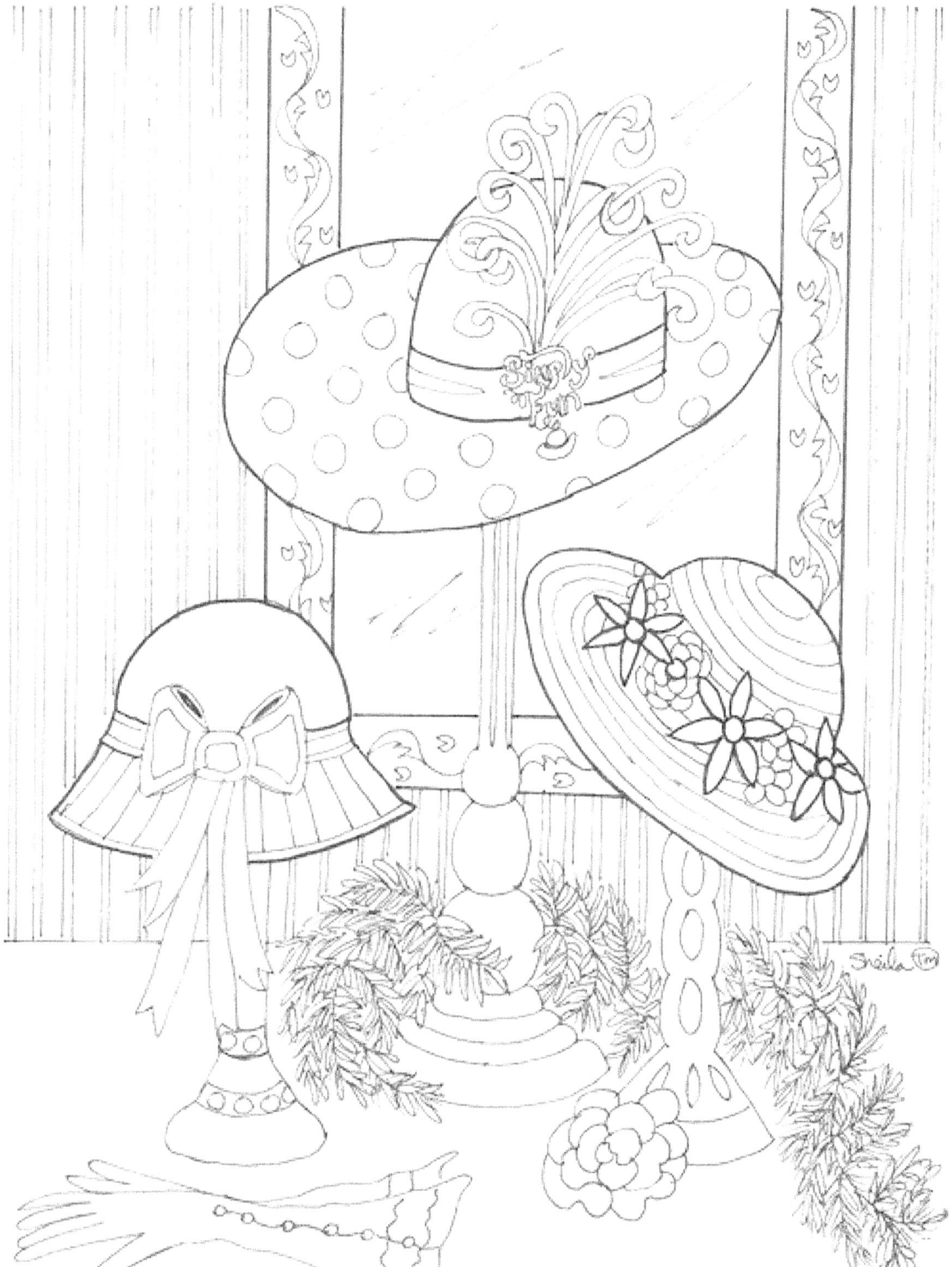
Sheila

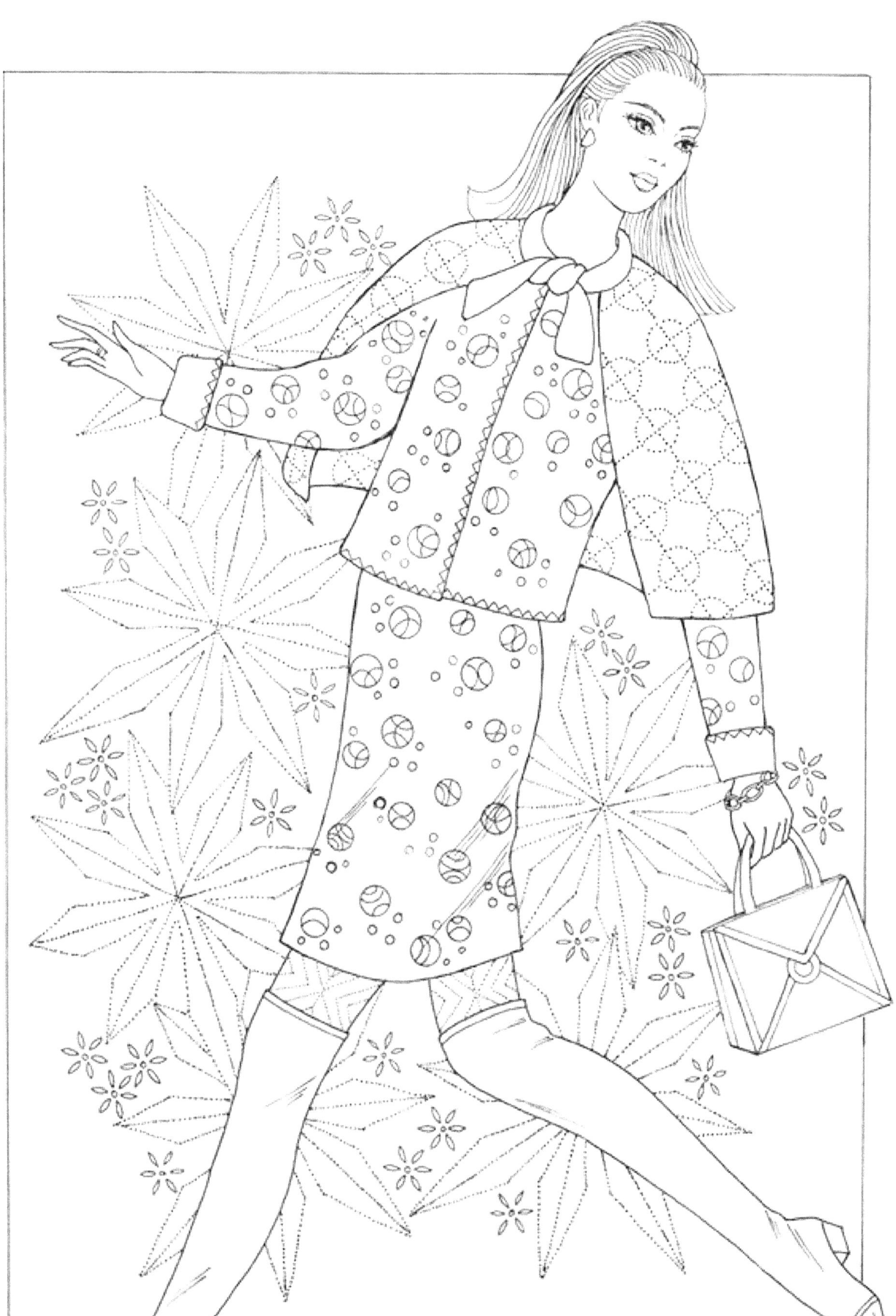

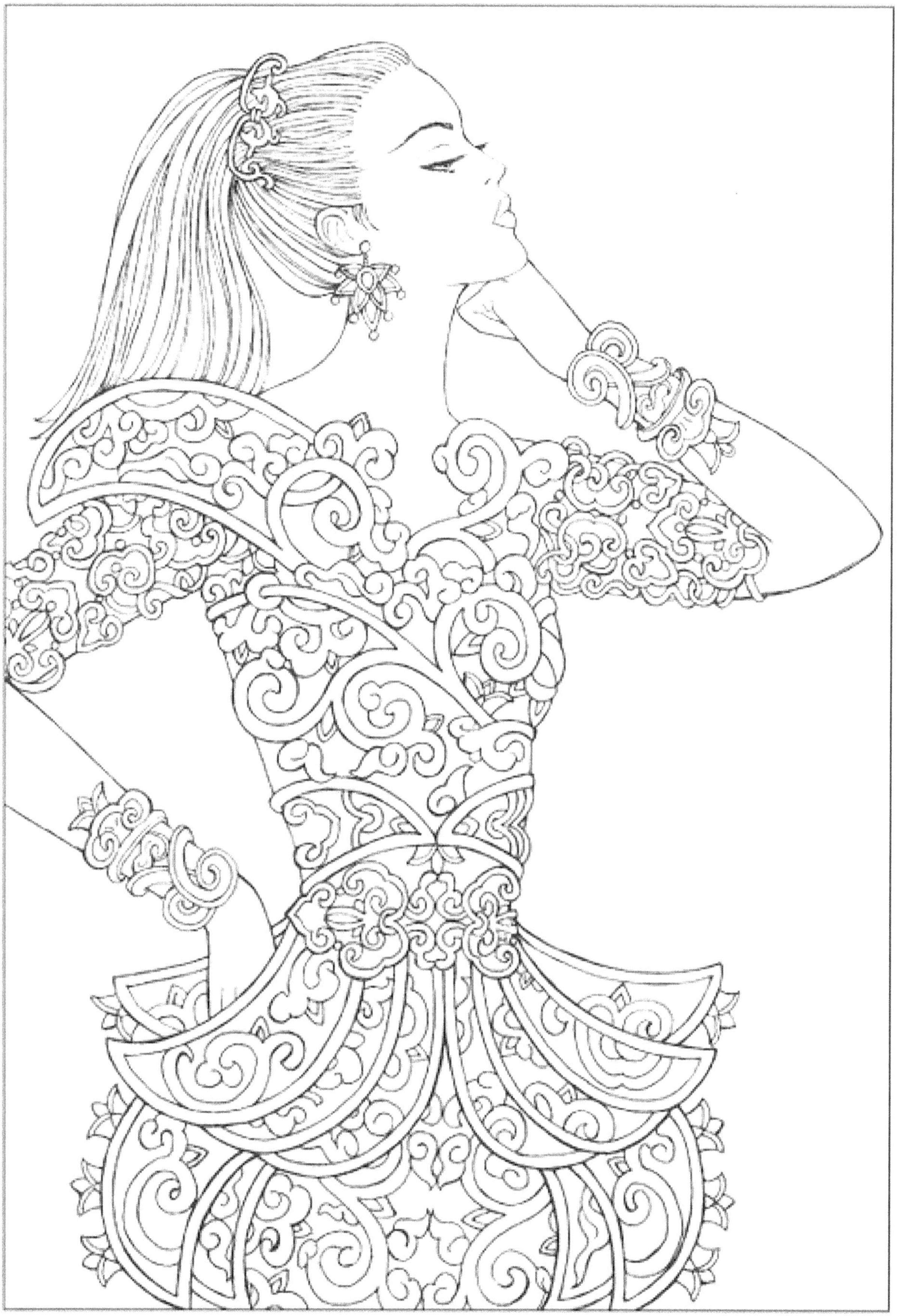

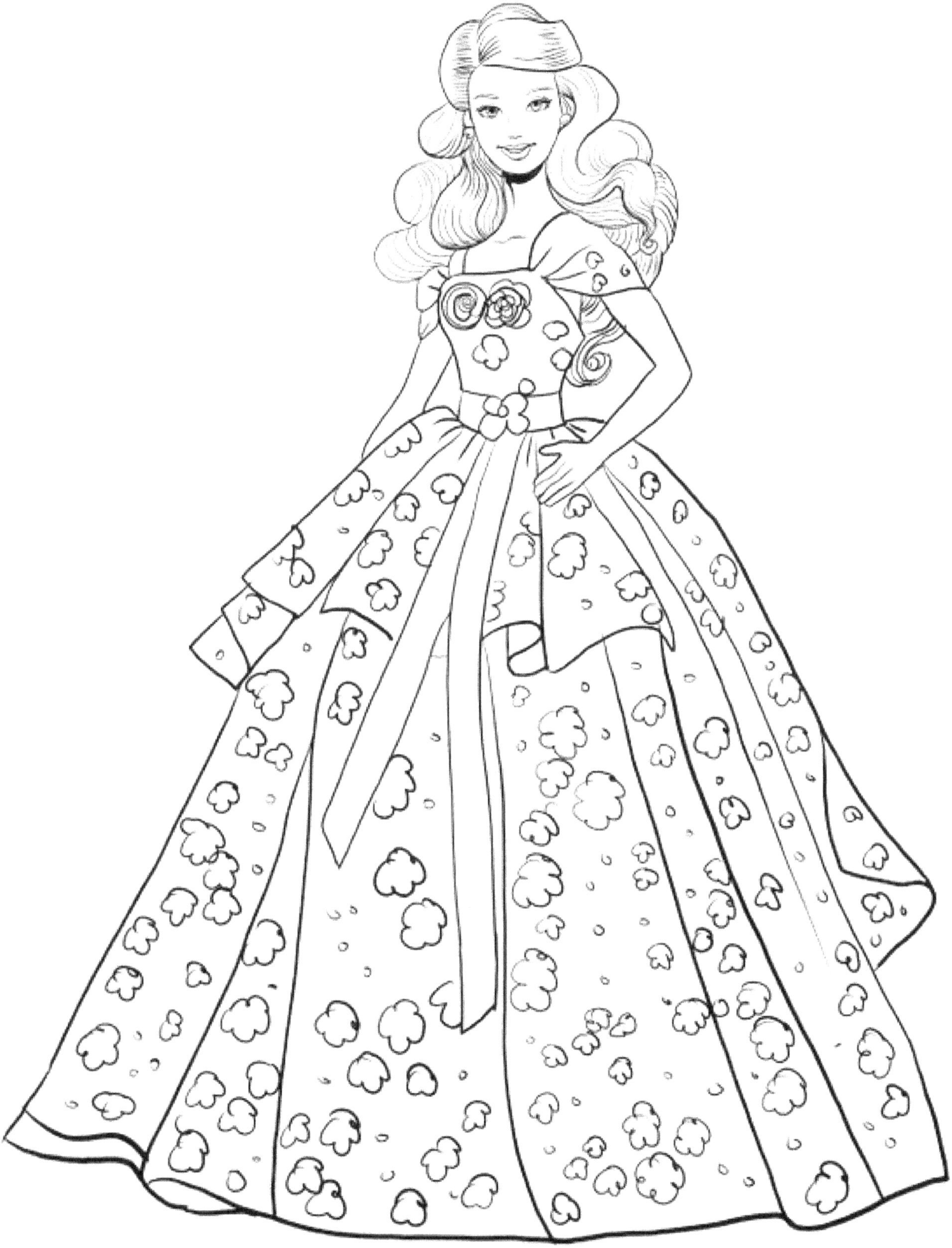

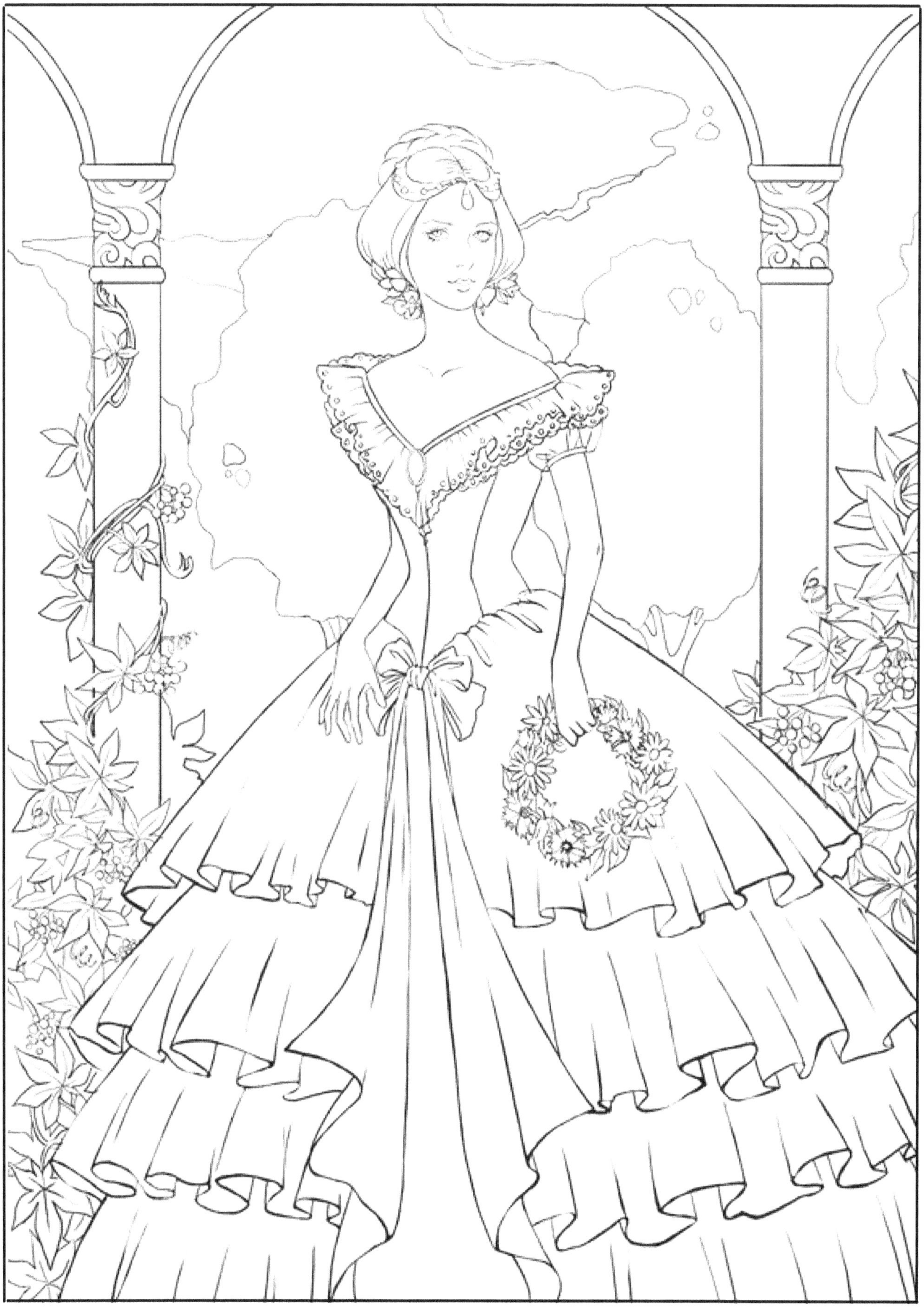

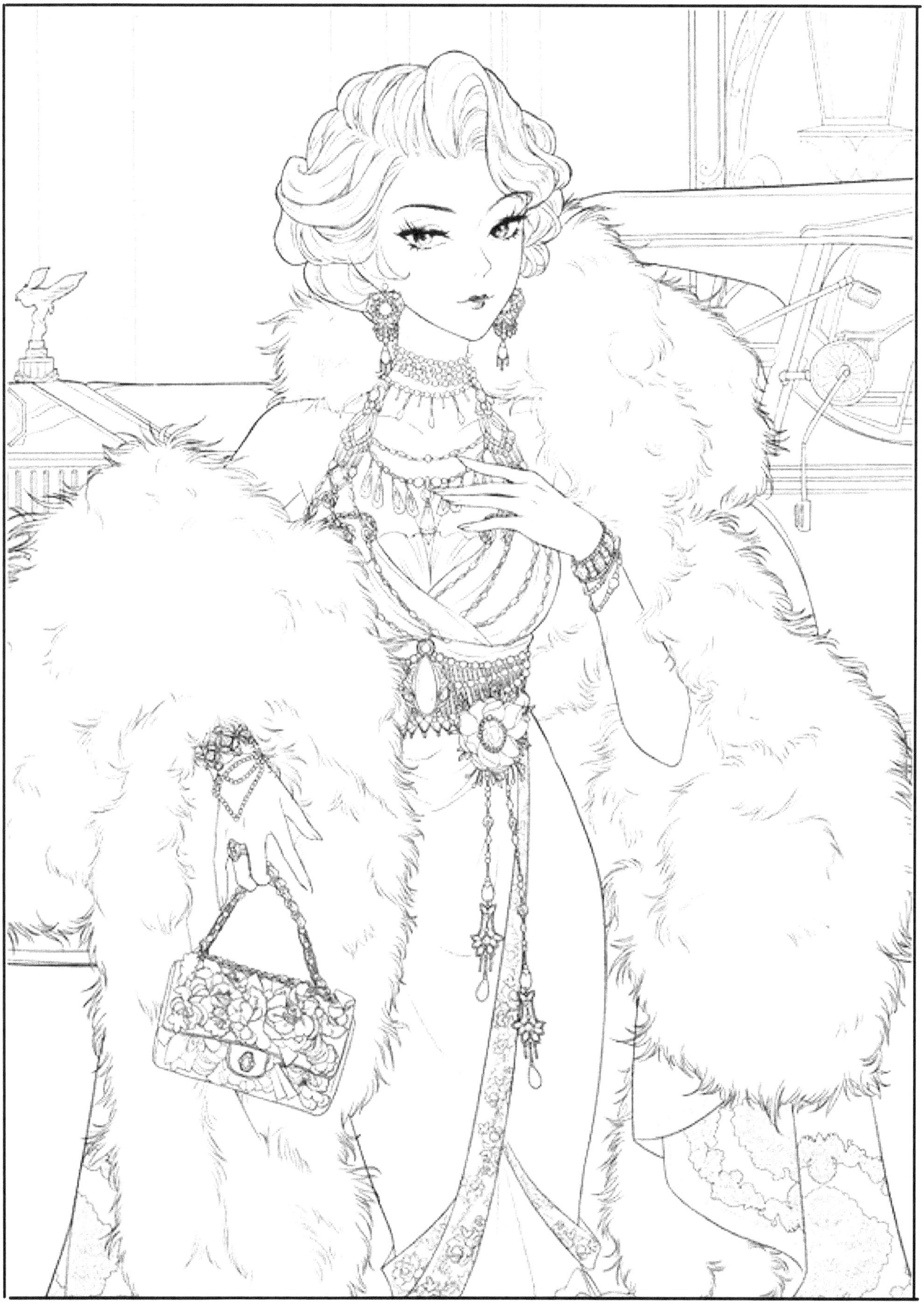

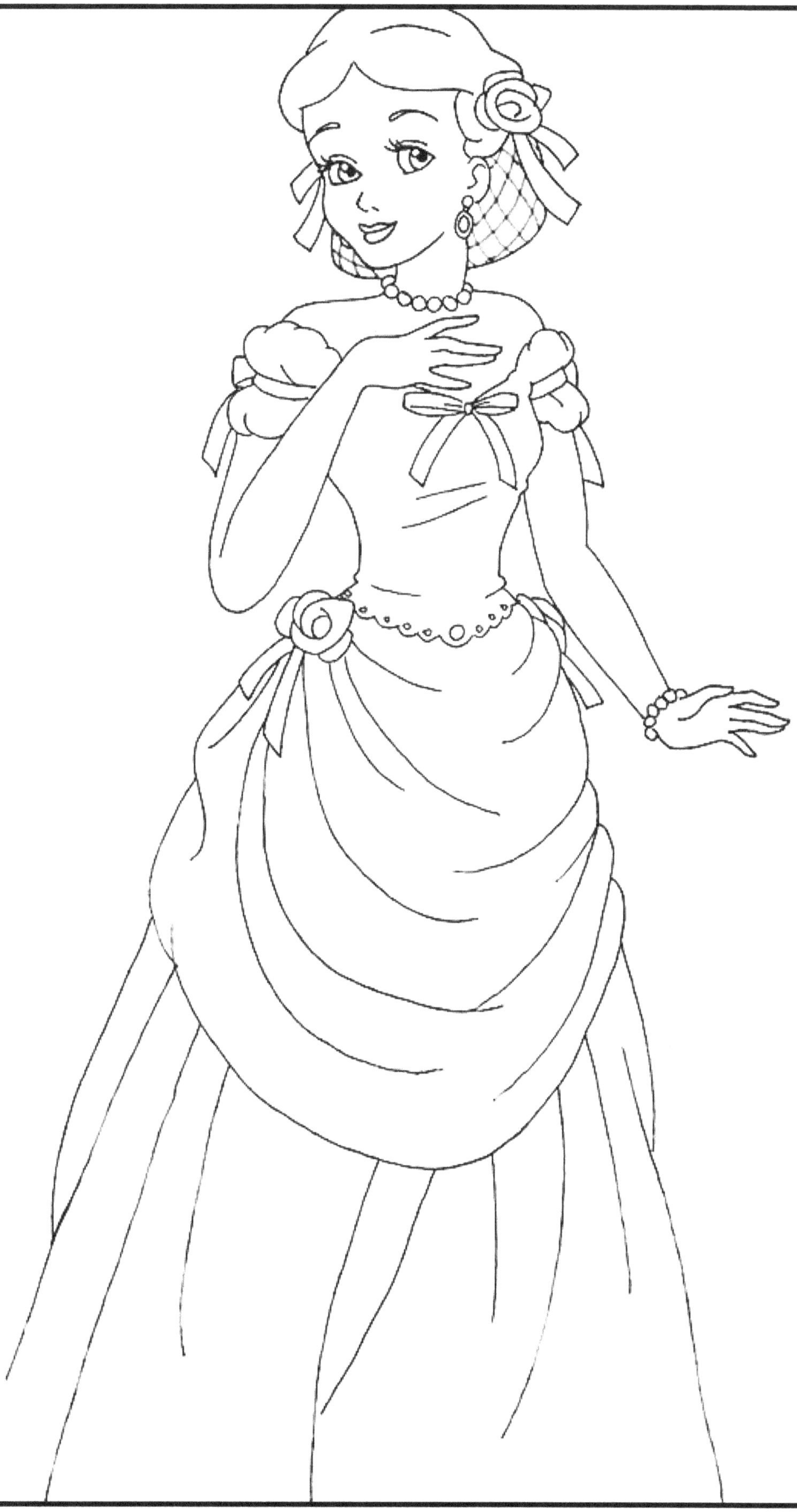

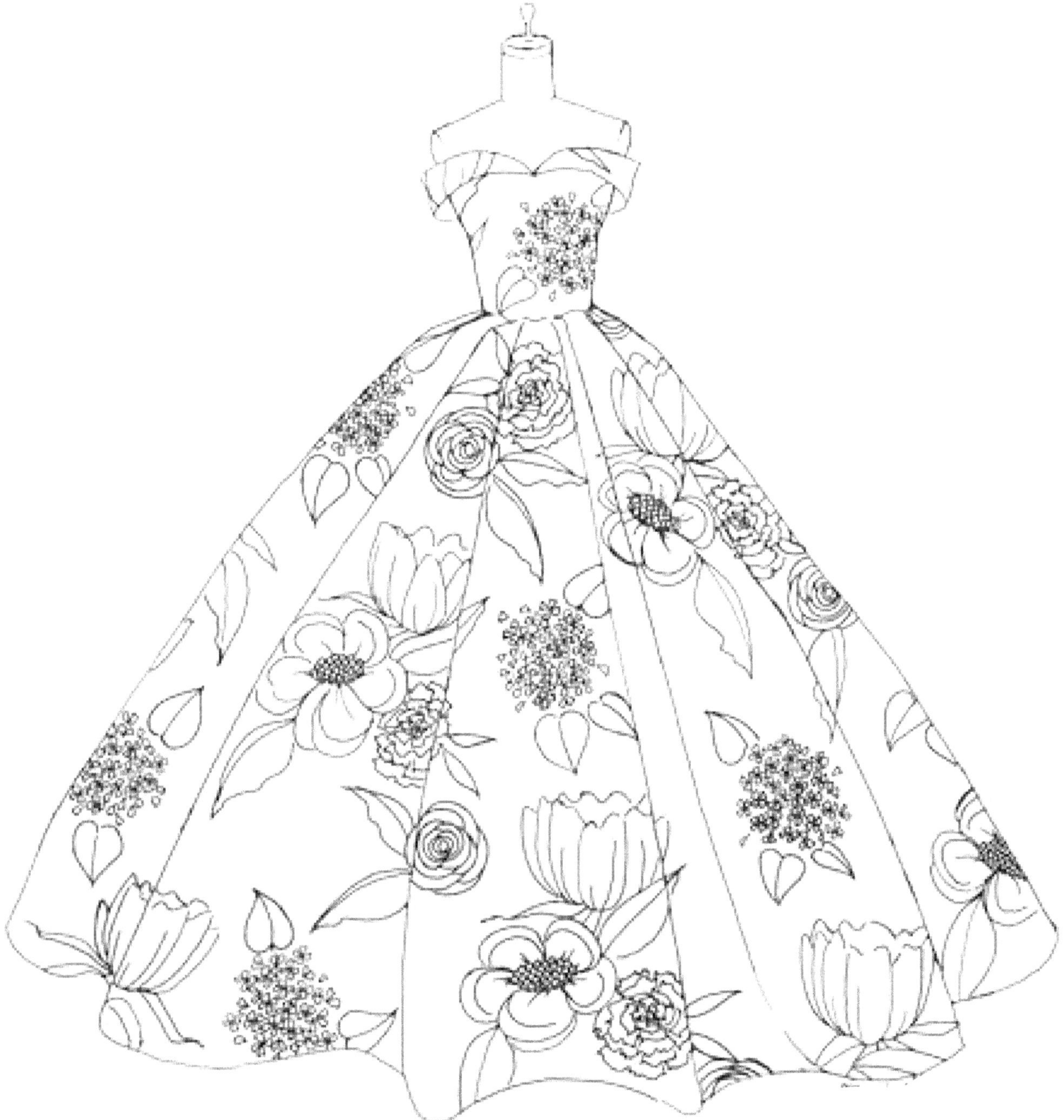

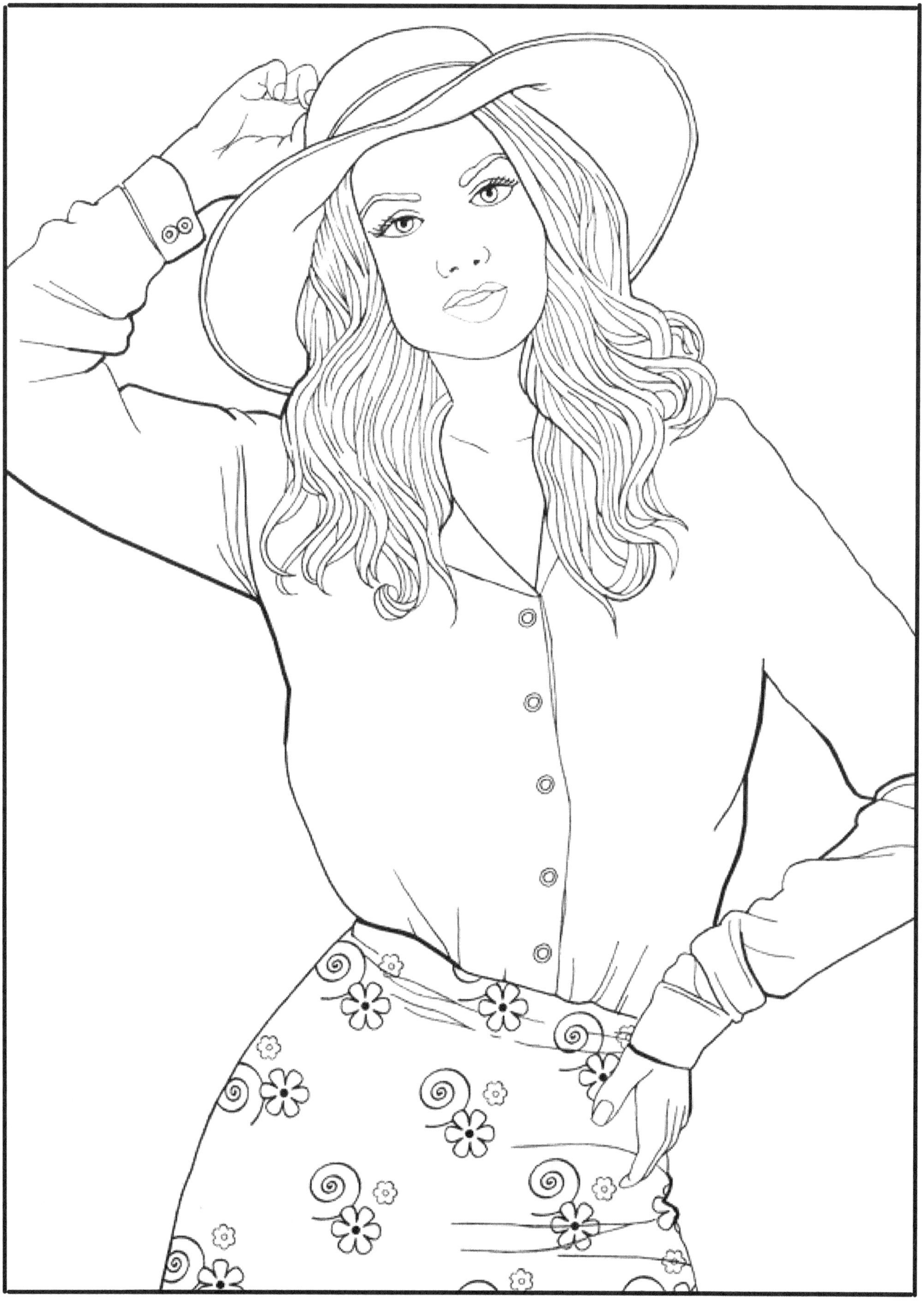

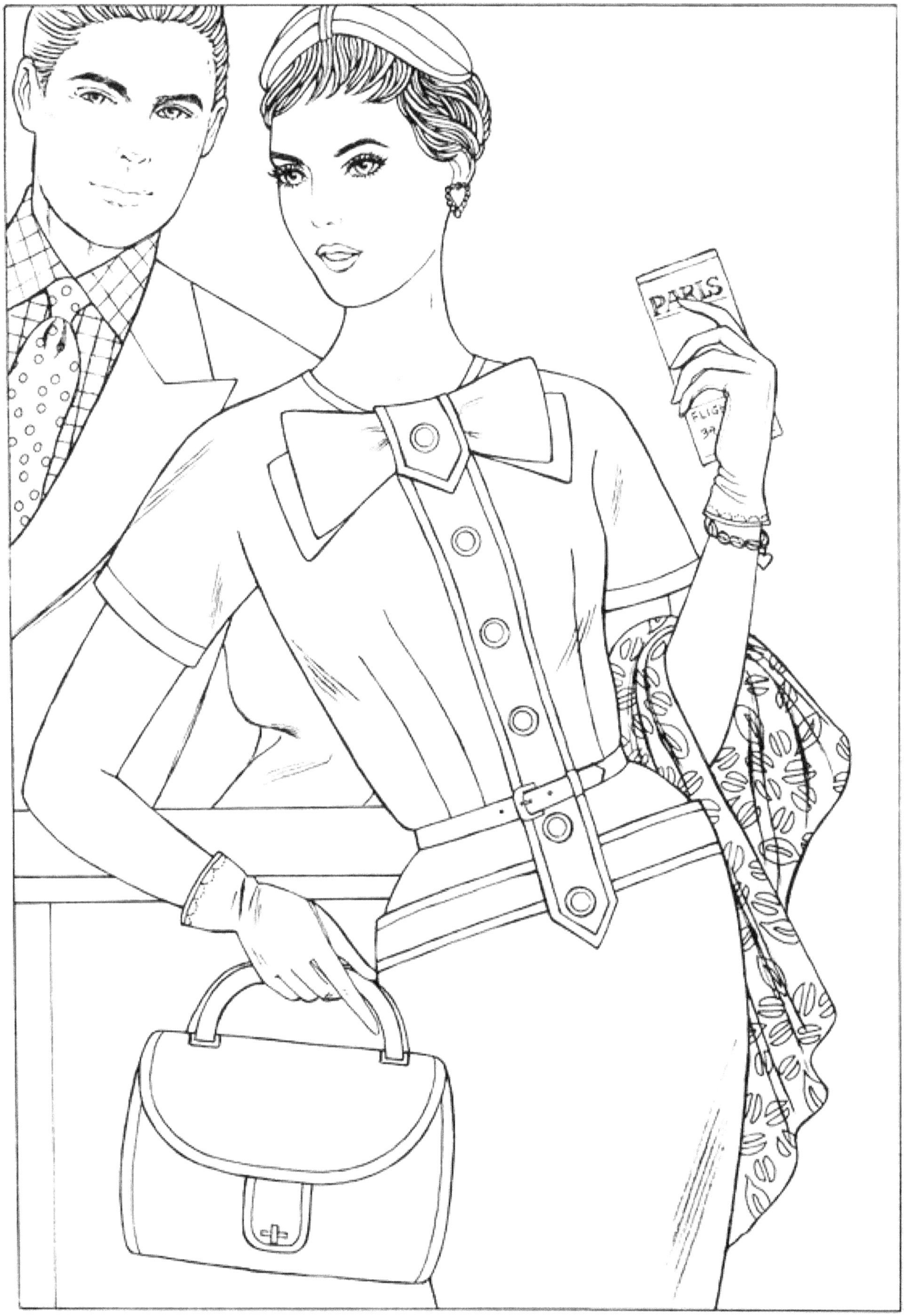
PARIS

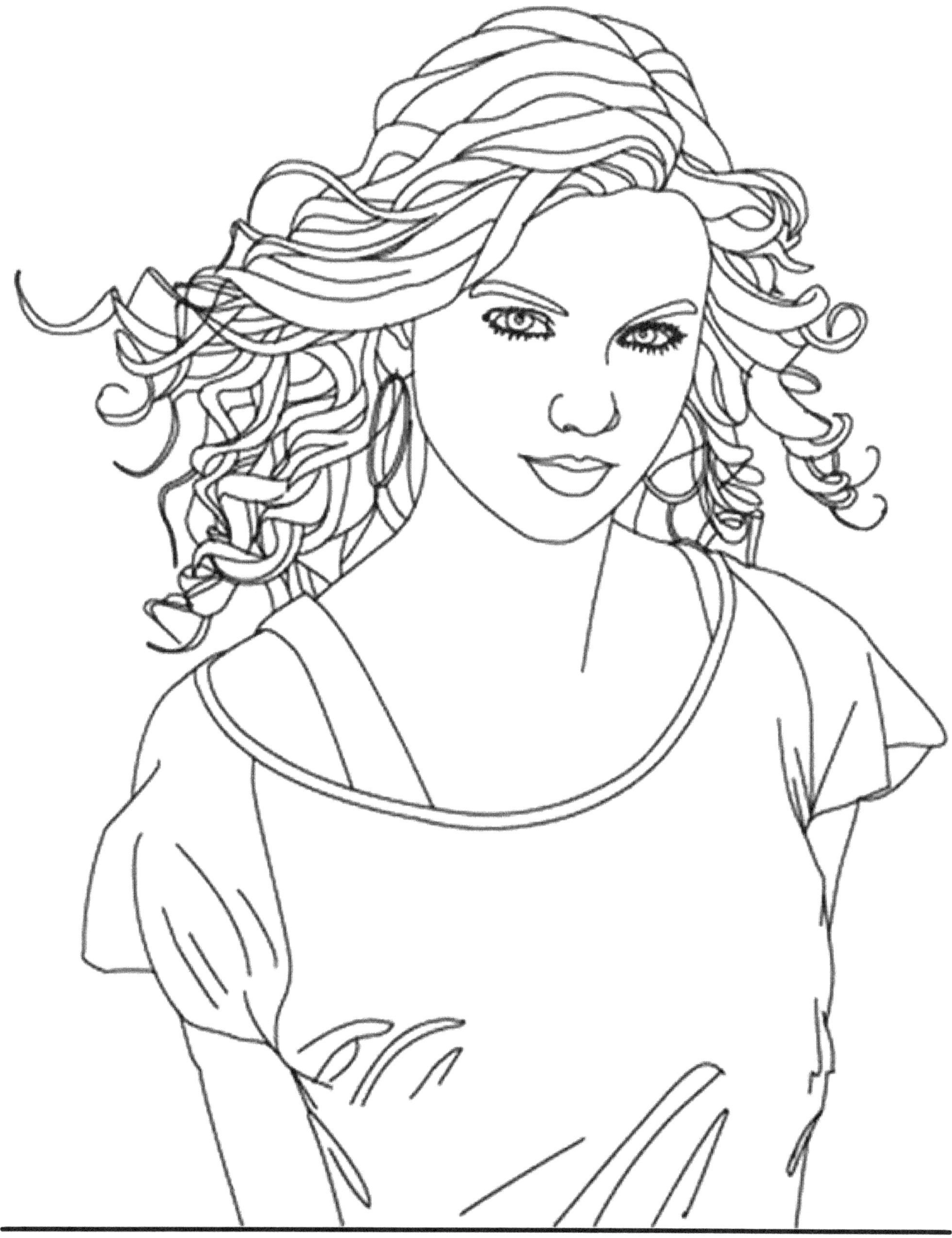

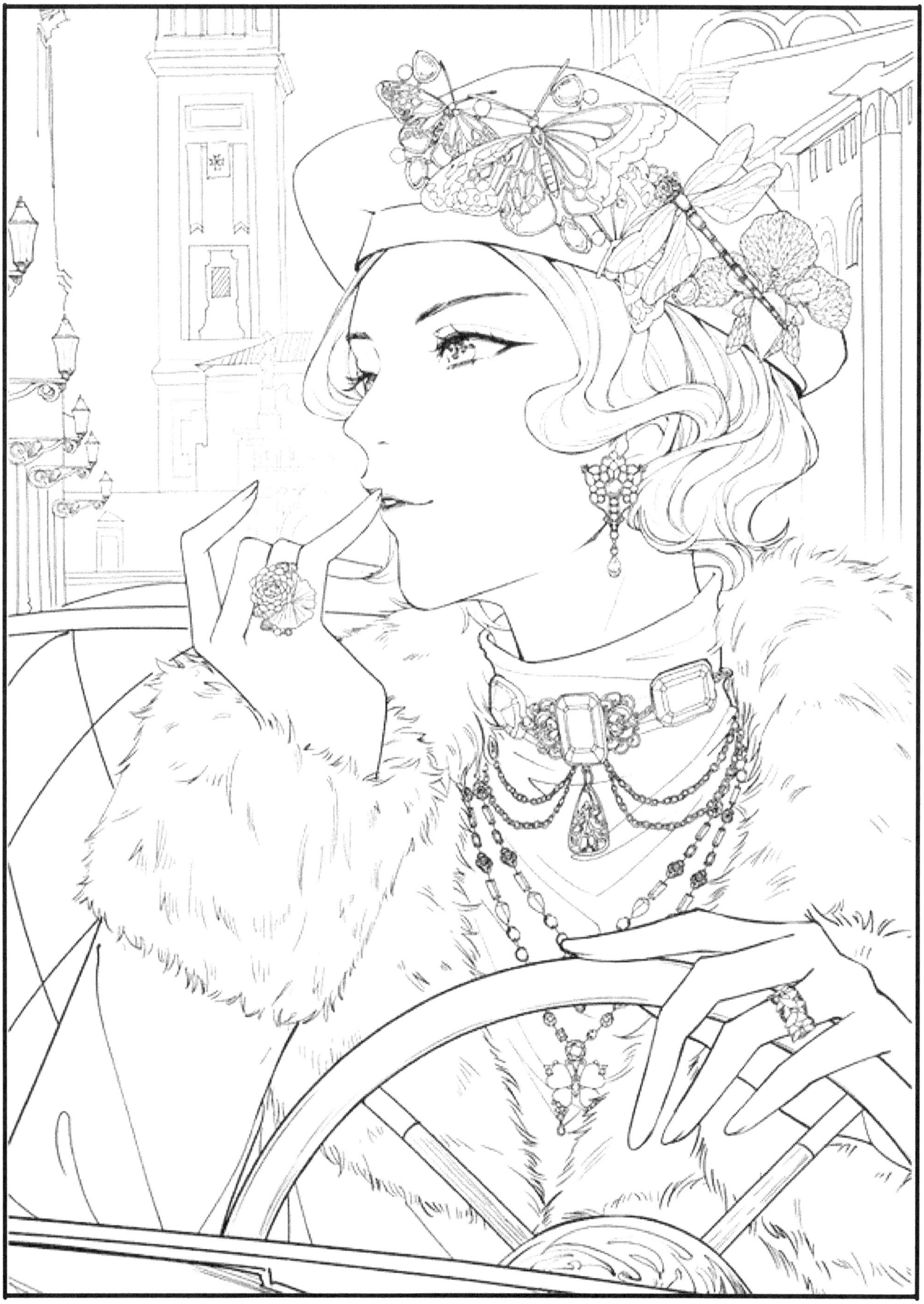

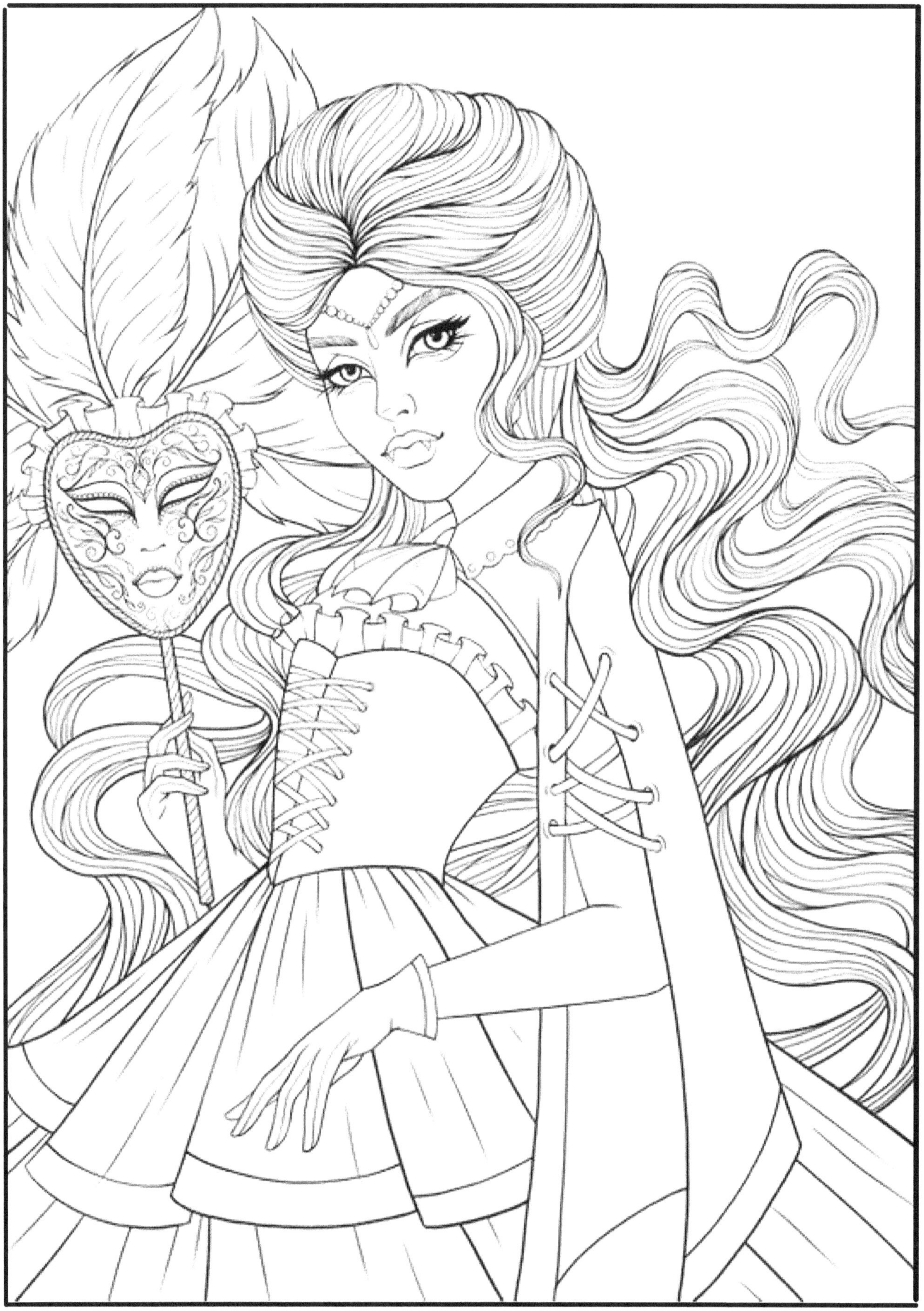

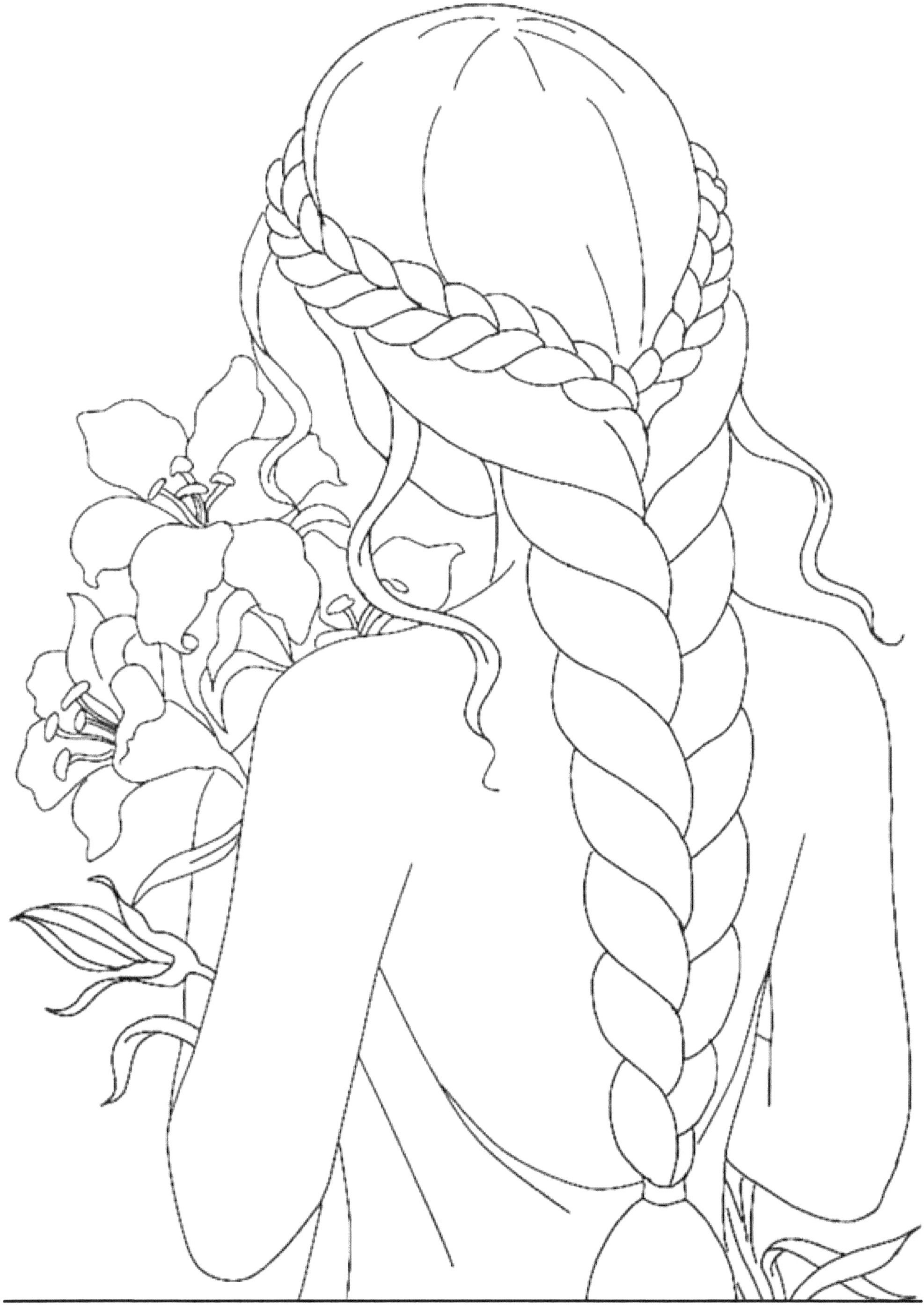

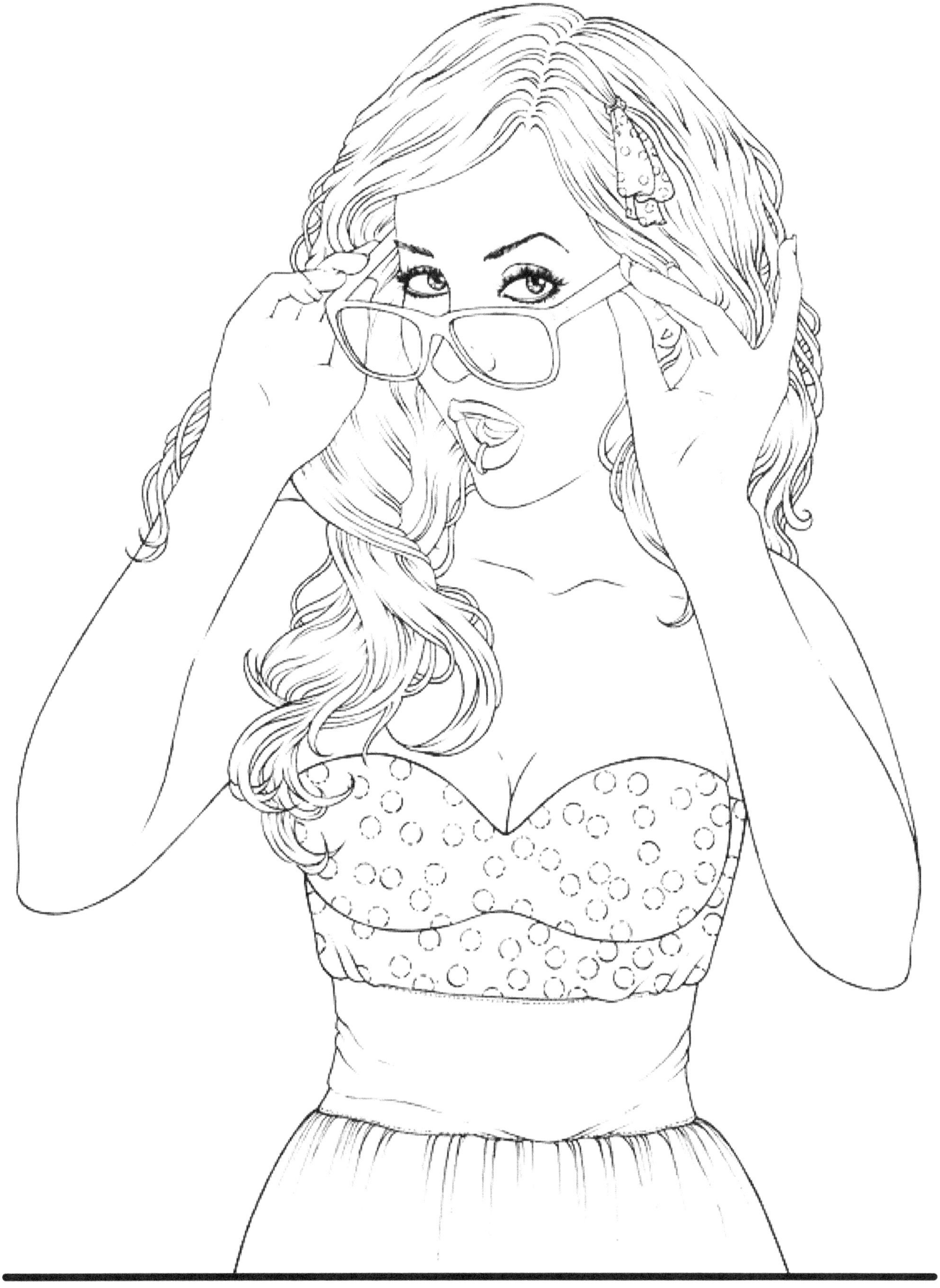

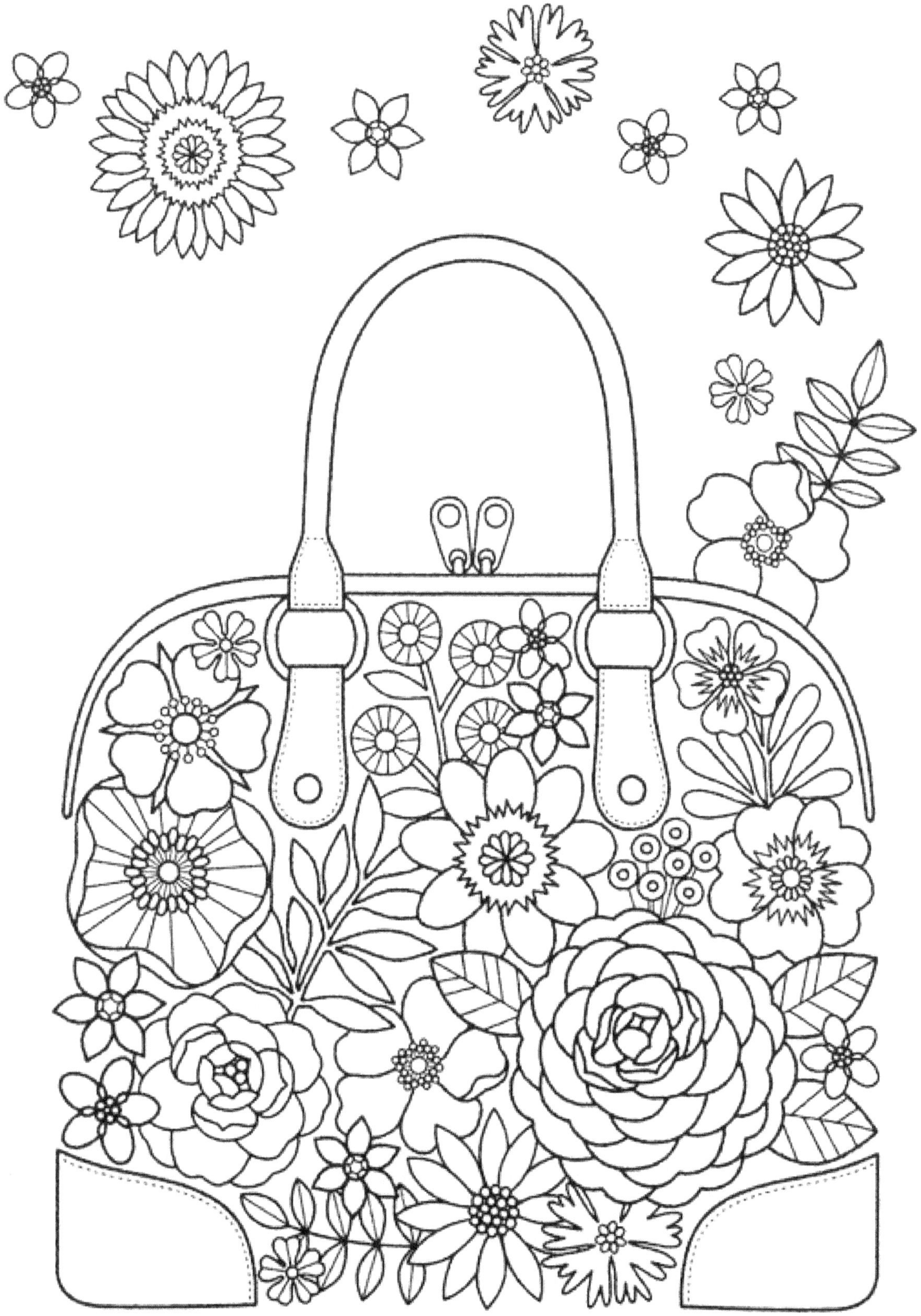

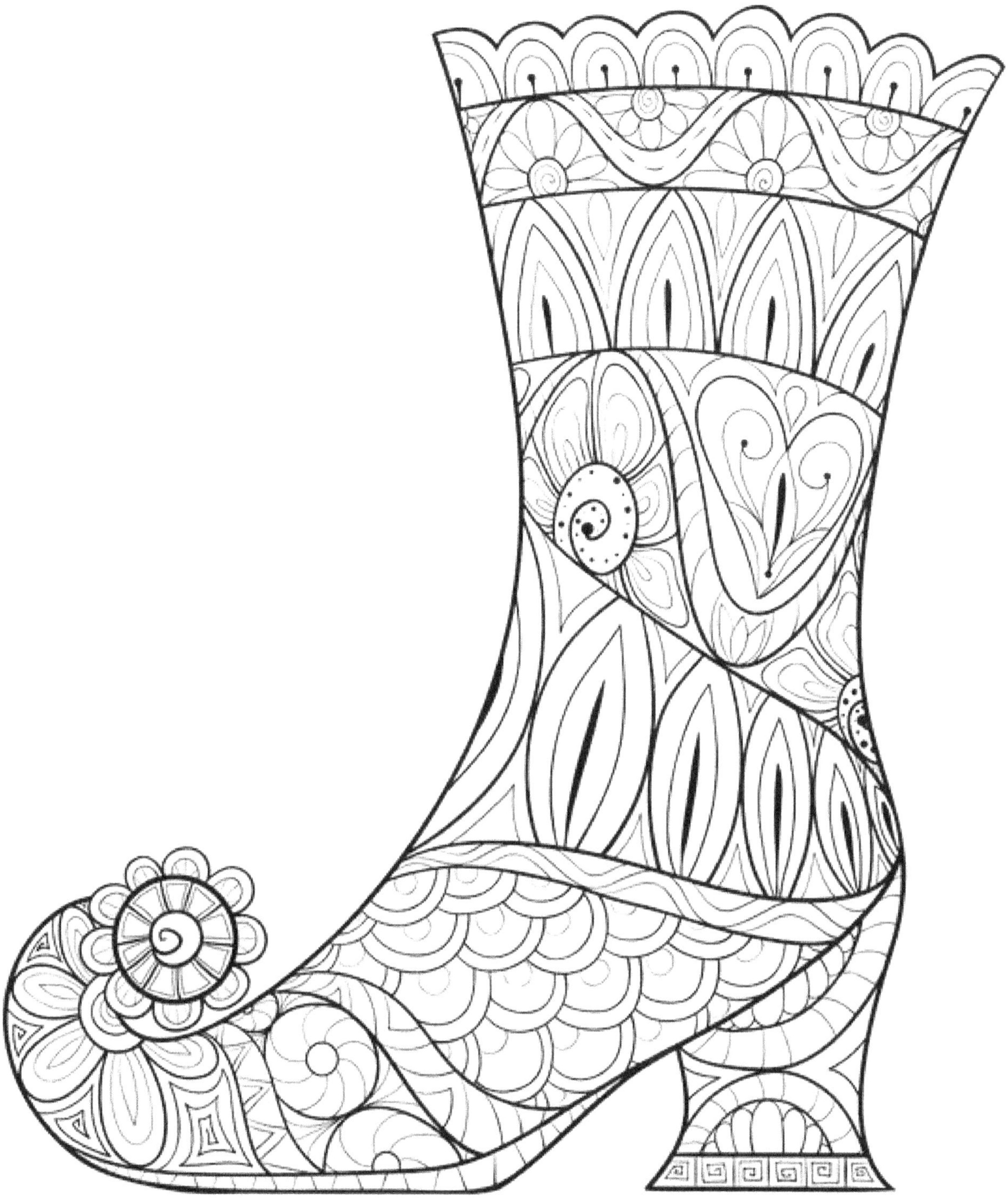

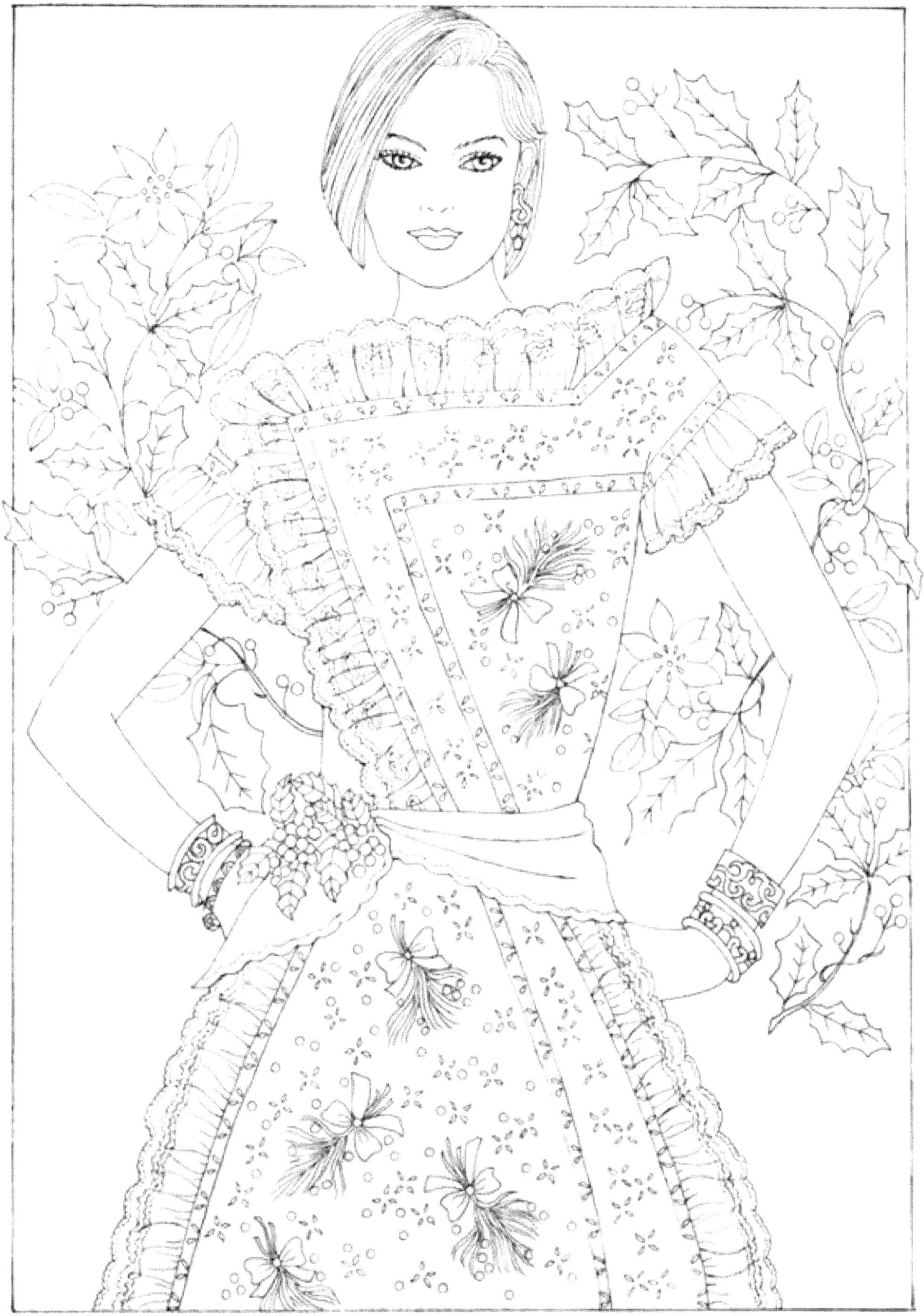

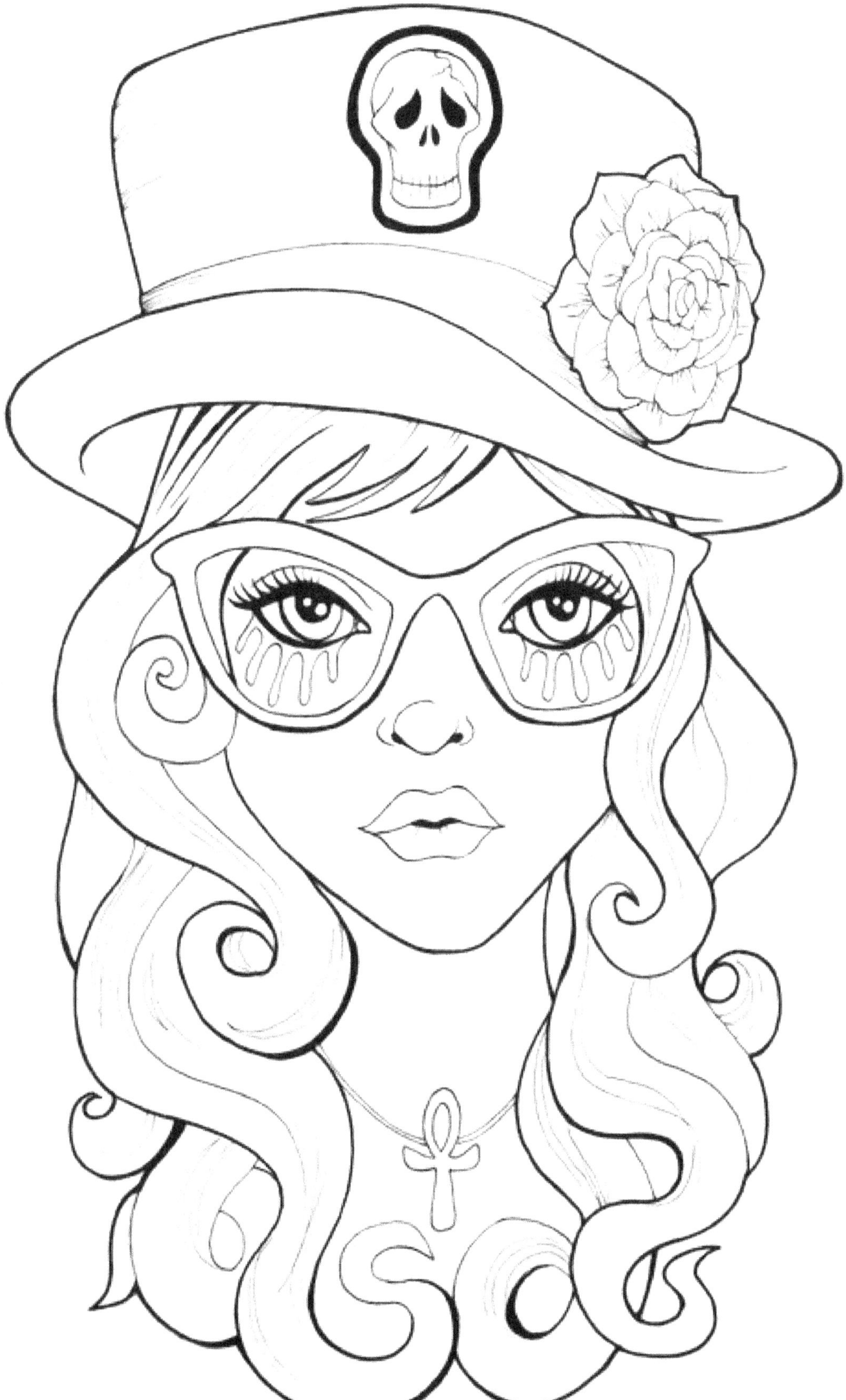

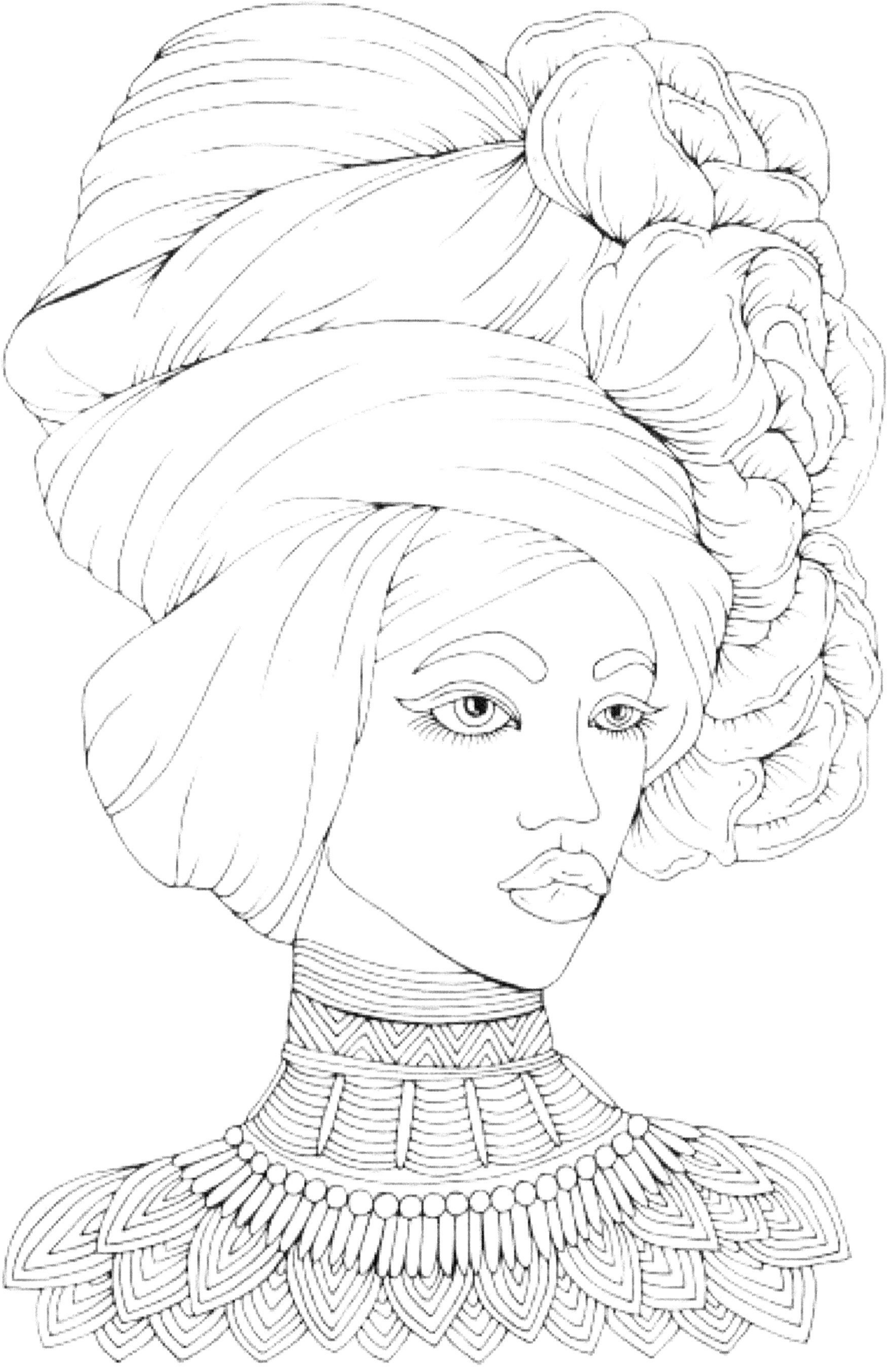

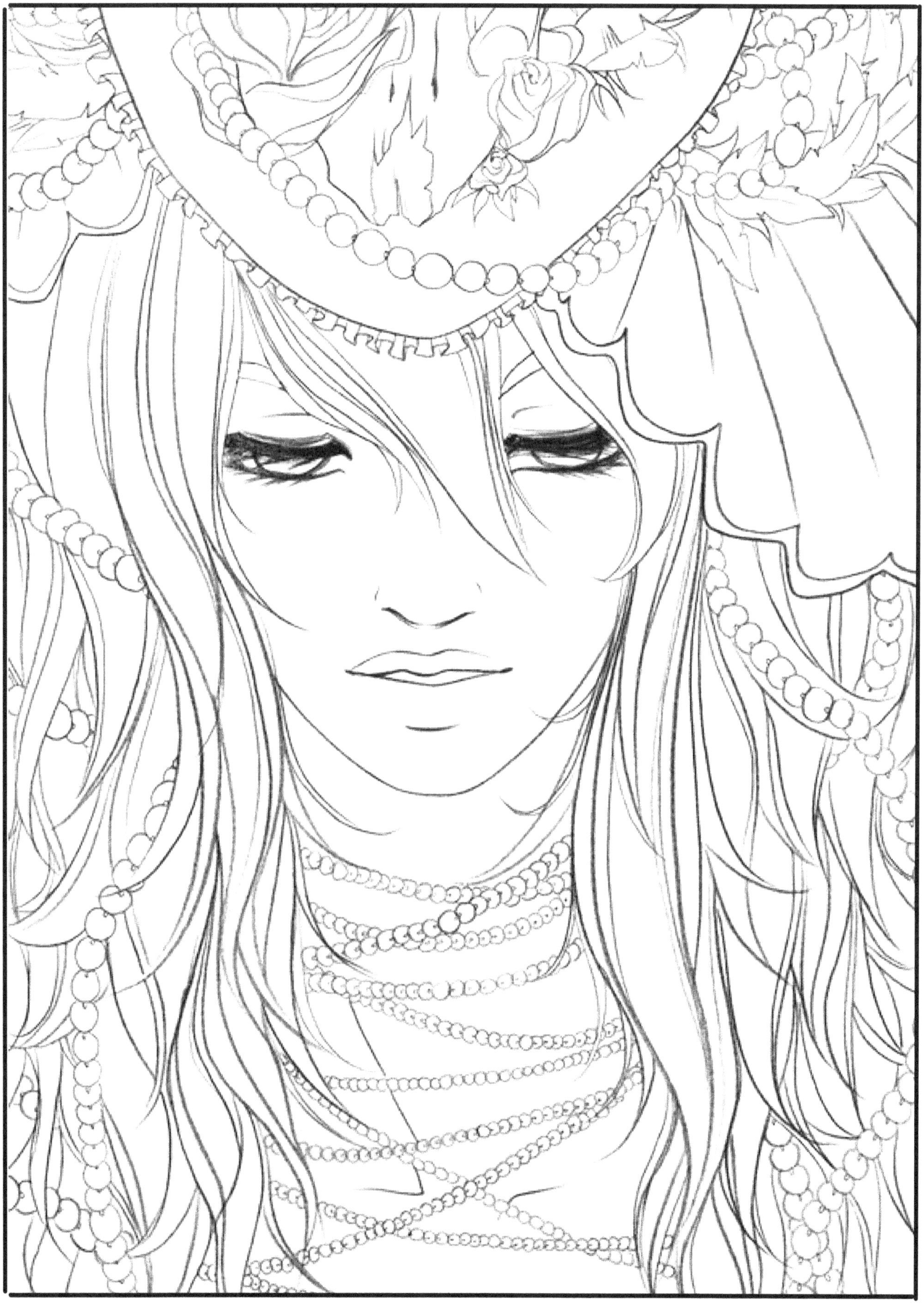

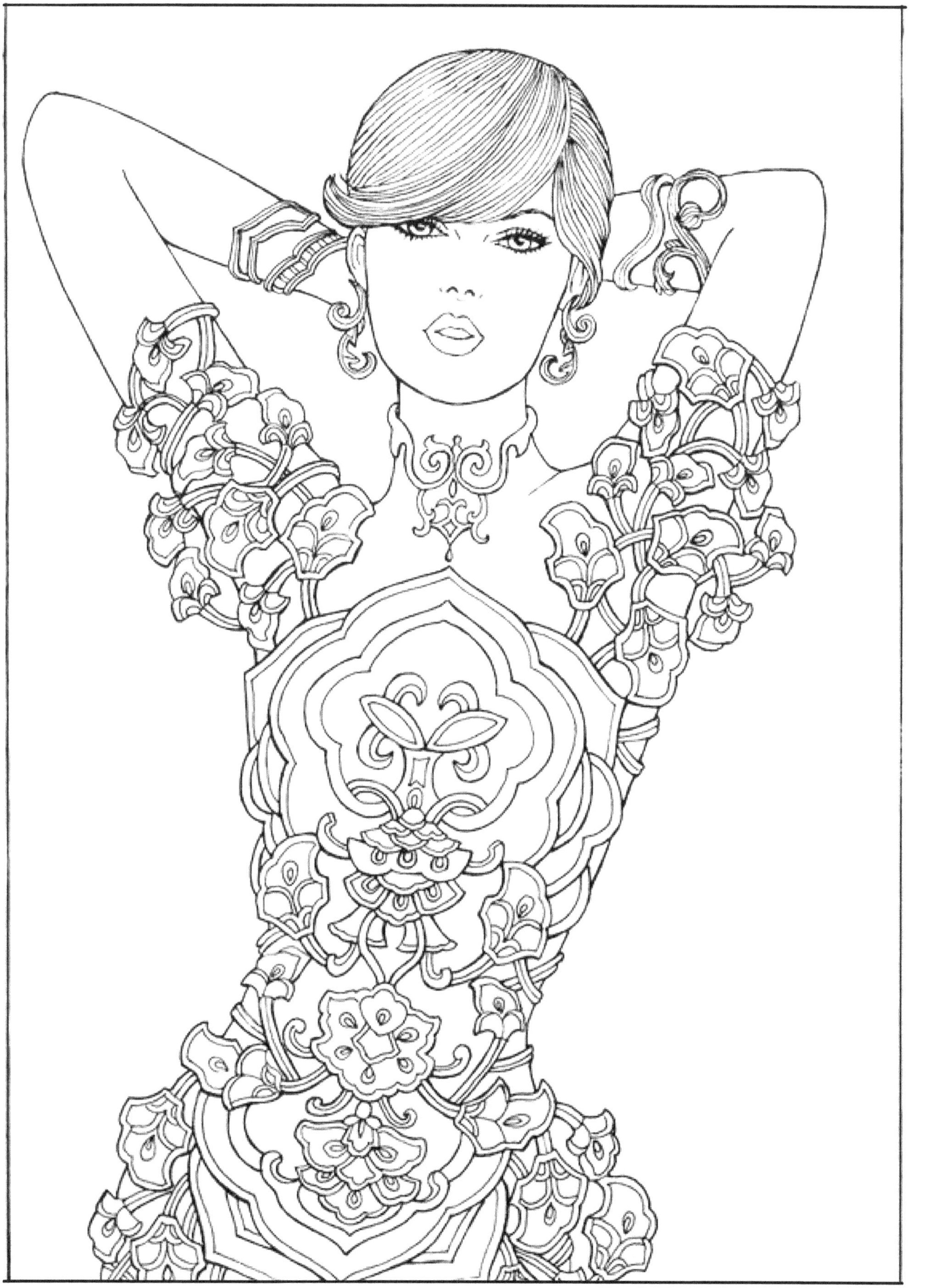

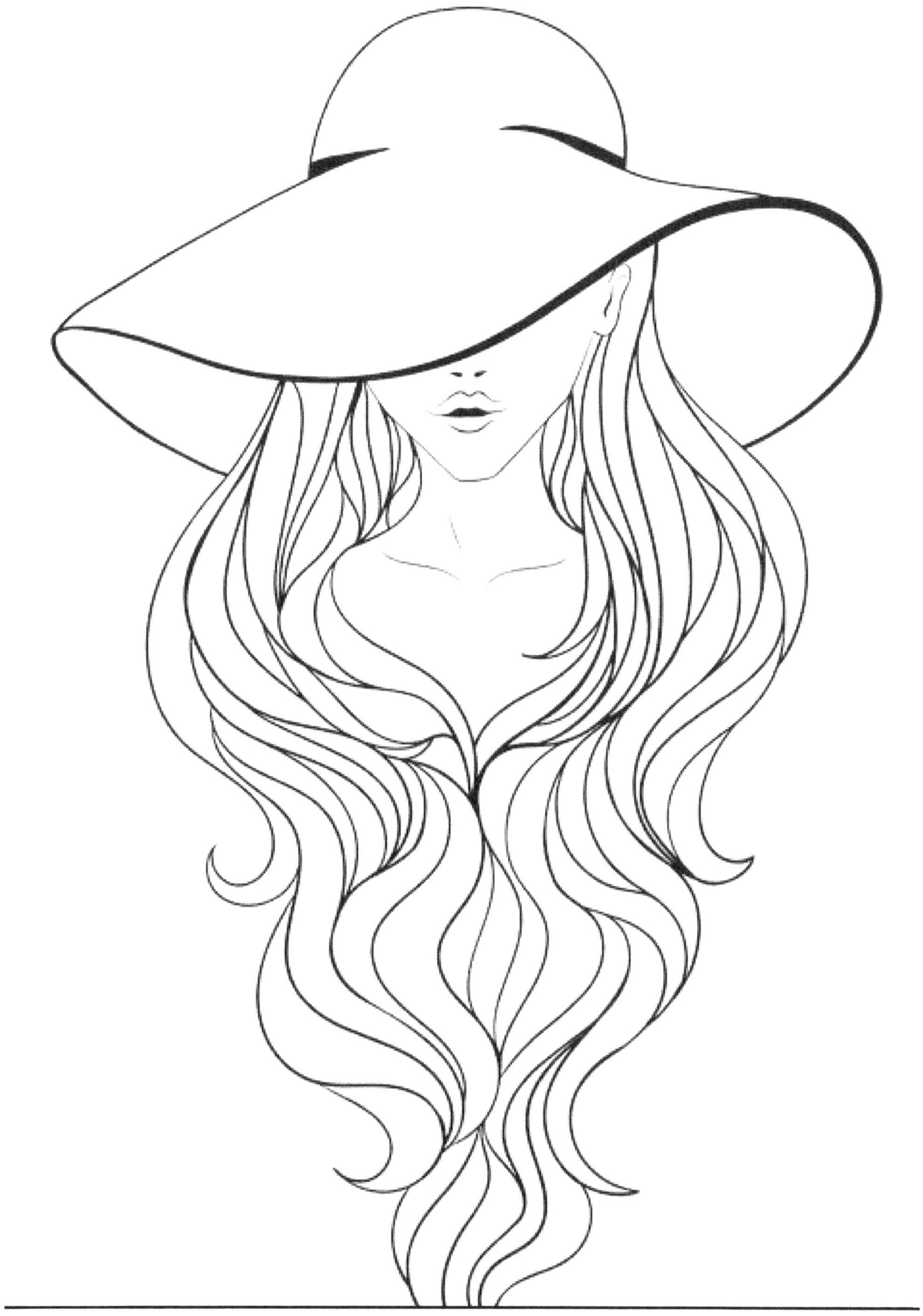

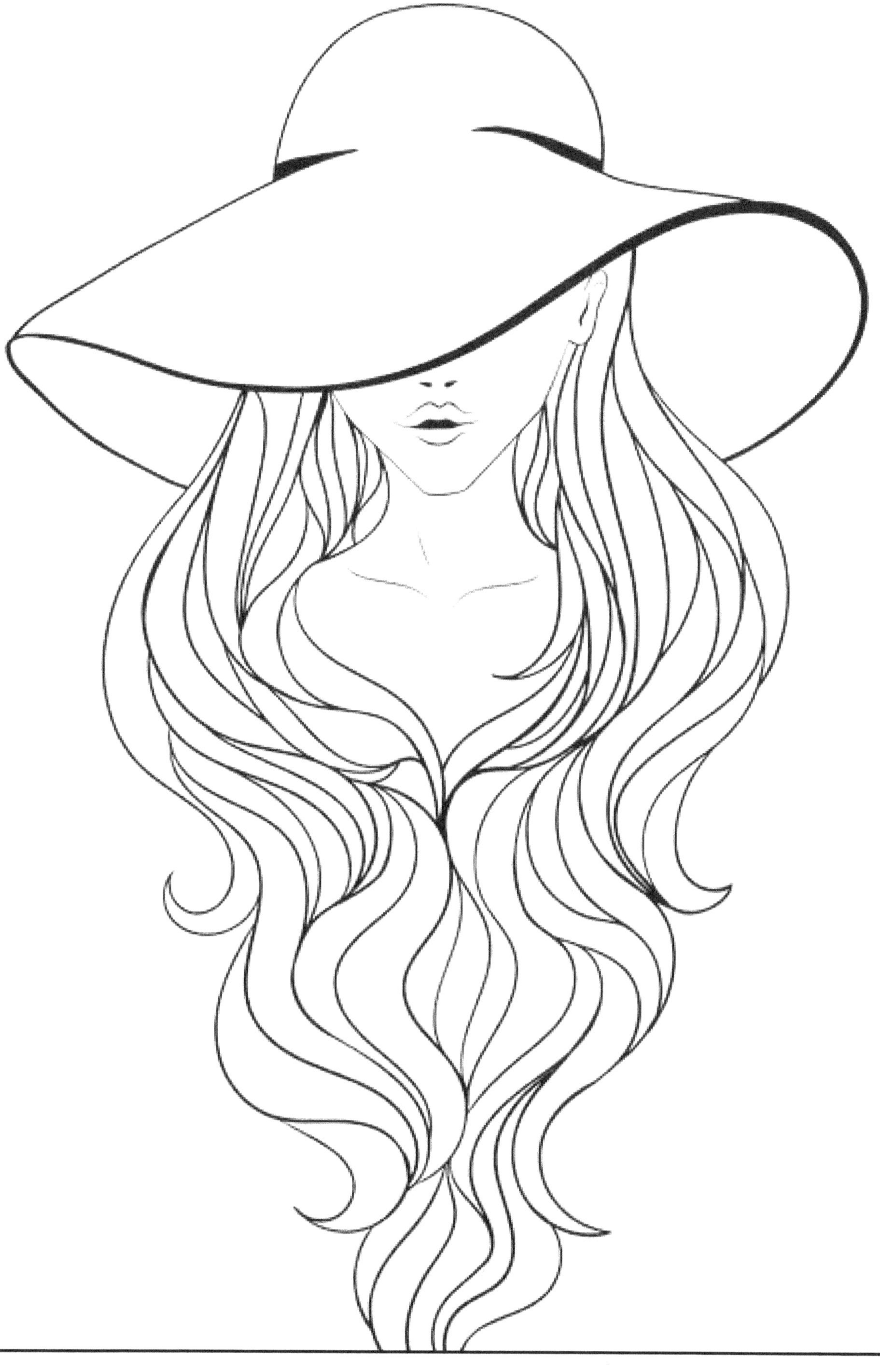

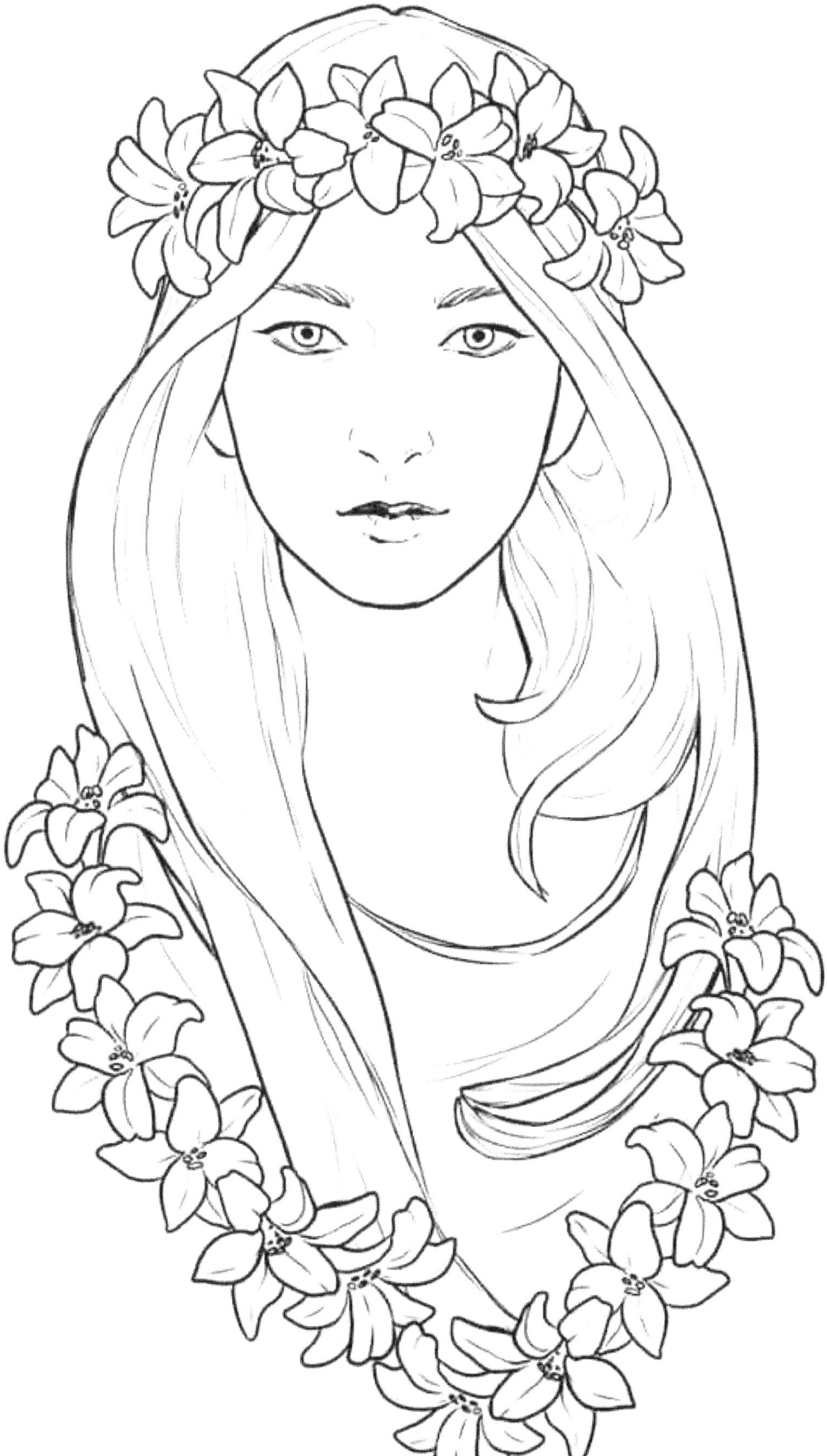

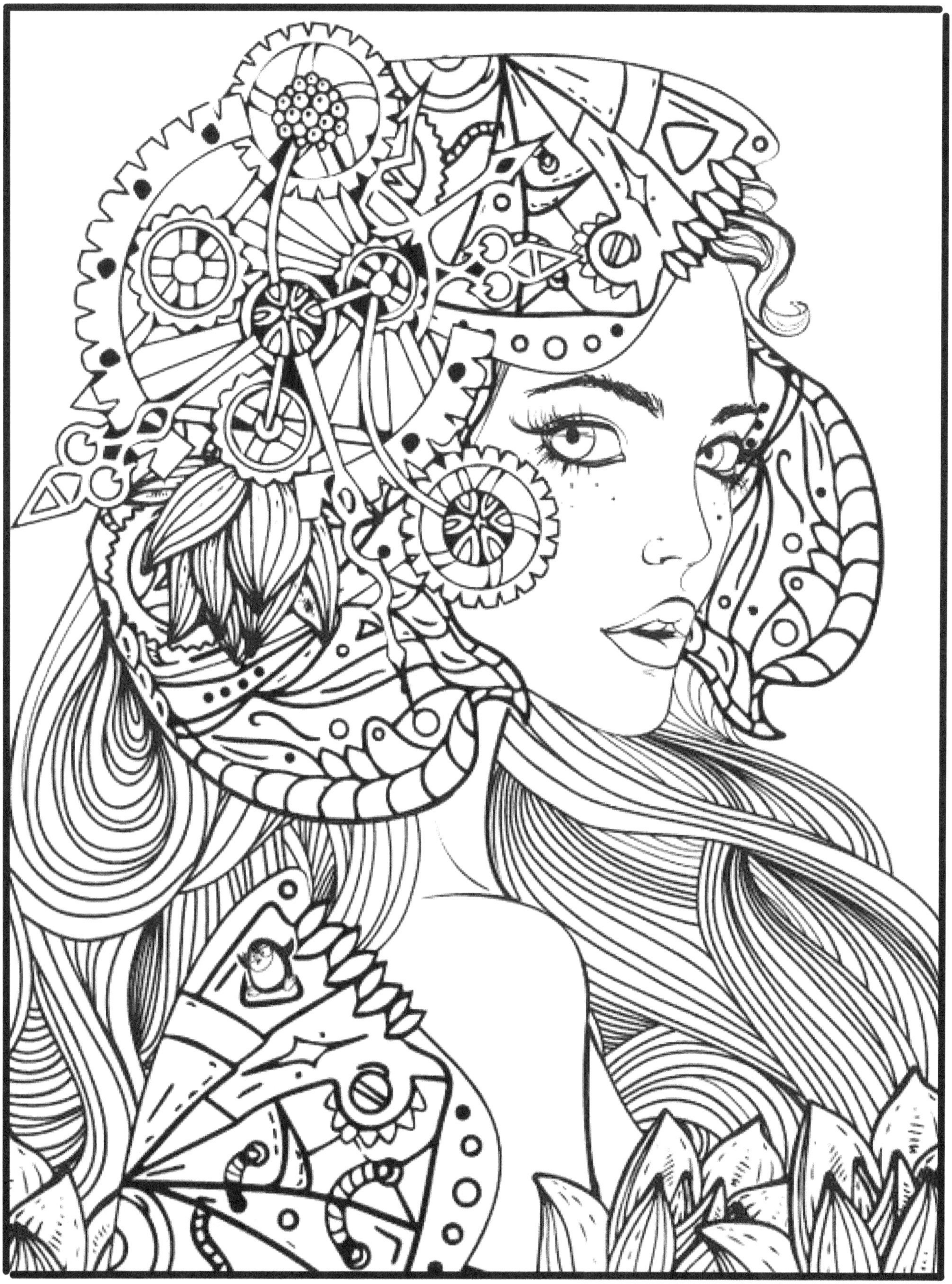

www.ingramcontent.com/pod-product-compliance
Lightning Source LLC
Chambersburg PA
CBHW080834220526
45467CB00008B/2274
* 9 7 9 8 7 1 8 1 0 9 0 8 5 *